Who do you say Jesus was?
Rebel? Fraud? Fake? Son of God?

The only way to find out is to walk with Jesus—to
experience his joys and sorrows, to learn of his
love and compassion, to witness his crucifixion
and his overwhelming triumph over death.

Based on the Gospel of Luke, and following the
screenplay of the new major motion picture of the
same name, JESUS allows you to walk as the
disciples did, in the footsteps of Jesus Christ.
Witness firsthand the centuries-old story, and
come face-to-face with a vibrant, winsome,
wondrous Person. Let this book unfold for you a
whole new dimension and add new life to the
inspiring story of Jesus.

Jesus

Lee Roddy

SPIRE BOOKS

FLEMING H. REVELL COMPANY
OLD TAPPAN, NEW JERSEY

This book tells the story of the film *Jesus* in words and pictures. The narrative is based on the scenario of the film.

ISBN 0-8007-8380-8

A Spire Book
Copyright © 1979 by Inspirational Film Distributors, Inc.
Published by Fleming H. Revell Company
All rights reserved
Library of Congress Catalog Card Number 79-67460
Printed in the United States of America

This is an original Spire book, published by Spire Books,
a Division of Fleming H. Revell Company,
Old Tappan, New Jersey

PROLOGUE

... because I have carefully studied all these matters from their beginning, I thought it would be good to write an orderly account for you. I do this so that you will know the full truth about everything which you have been taught.

Luke 1:3, 4

FOREWORD

About forty years after Jesus was crucified, buried, and rose from the dead, a Greek physician named Luke took writing instruments in hand and began the first of a two-part volume with these words:

Dear Theophilus:

Many people have done their best to write a report of the things that have taken place among us. They wrote what we have been told by those who saw these things from the beginning and who proclaimed the message. And so, Your Excellency, because I have carefully studied all these matters from their beginning, I thought it would be good to write an orderly account for you. I do this so that you will know the full truth about everything which you have been taught.

The full truth. That was the purpose Luke had in writing to an unknown official, presumably a Gentile, who was friendly to the rapidly spreading Christian faith.

There were various accounts circulating at the time, however, and Luke saw the need for a carefully investigated, chronologically recorded report on the life of this one man, Jesus. So Luke set himself to the task of personally investigating everything from the beginning and systematically writing his conclusion.

His opening remarks suggest Luke sought out eyewitnesses and asked for their account, as he pursued this investigation. Finally, having researched the whole story of Jesus' life from before He was born, until the risen Christ ascended into heaven, Luke began writing a letter. In his time, that was the only medium available to him.

Today, there are other media for telling the "full truths" of the Jesus story. One such medium is film. It was with this medium that John Heyman, a movie producer and a Christian of Jewish heritage, sought to tell the unvarnished story of Jesus. In the process of producing the film, John was often asked, "Why are you doing a film about Jesus?" He invariably answered, "Because it's never been done before."

And John was right. For although there have been many feature films on the life of Christ, not one has been totally faithful to the Scriptures—not one, that is, until now.

Being totally faithful to Scripture was one of the criteria John Heyman established before making *Jesus*. He wanted a film that was totally accurate and completely authentic. He handed the Gospel of Luke to a scenarist with the words, "Here is the script. I want you to put it in scene form." And the writer did. Over 95 percent of the content of *Jesus* is taken directly from Saint Luke's Gospel. In the film, Jesus speaks only the words recorded in the Gospel of Luke. *Jesus* truly is the authentic story from the only authentic source.

And, through the film and this book, it is the hope of those involved that the story of Jesus will enrich the lives of thousands of people who earnestly desire to know more about the Man who changed the course of history—and who can transform their lives.

J. D. KENNETH BLISS
President, Inspirational
Films

Before you begin:

The movie *Jesus* and the book *Jesus* are more than a simple retelling of the story from the Gospel of St. Luke. *Jesus*, the movie, is worthy of being studied and discussed in depth because of its consistent harmony with Luke's Gospel. However, the film is not intended as a replacement for the incomparable Word of God. Hopefully, any readers of this book and viewers of the movie who have specific questions will turn to the only authentic source for their answers: THE BIBLE.

CHAPTER ONE

Two youths hurried along the narrow, rocky road, urging the small, brown donkey with soft, urgent voices. A moment before, the older one, a teenage Jew with just the beginnings of a dark, curly beard, had spotted a furtive movement in the rocks high to the right of the Judean road.

"Someone's waiting for us," the youth said, pulling nervously at his black, curling hair. He wore the long cotton shirt, which fell to midcalf, a leather girdle at the waist, and an old goat-hair cloak, which was too long for his stubby five-foot frame.

"I know," his companion answered. He was barely fourteen, with a trace of dark upper lip. He also wore the same dress as his older companion—garments which marked them as people of the land.

They urged the donkey ahead with sharp slaps on either side of his rough, brown hide. Neither youth looked at the load of firewood creaking on the beast's sturdy back. Underneath that wood, where a casual eye would not see it, was a rolled parchment.

The older boy's brown eyes searched the huge limestone formations and rock outcroppings, where the unknown danger waited. He tried not to turn his head but used his eyes like spears to thrust into the shadows. He could see nothing.

"Could be Roman soldiers," he said, trying to sound cheerful.

"Or Sicarii," his companion replied. His voice cracked slightly with the terror the word brought.

The older youth shook his dark head and tugged so urgently on the donkey's woven camel-hair lead-rope that the beast jerked his long muzzle up in surprise at the unaccustomed force.

"I don't think so. Sicarii are urban fighters. They wouldn't be out in the country. Besides, they only wait to stick their daggers into Romans or very Hellenized Jews. We don't look like either."

"Bandits, then," the younger one said, admitting his fears. "We shouldn't have come alone."

"We had no choice," his friend whispered. They were drawing near the place where the road narrowed and the movement had been seen.

"We could have waited," the other youth said plaintively. "Nobody with any sense travels this country, except in a caravan."

"There was no choice," his friend repeated, emphasizing the words with a low vehemence. "They're waiting for that parchment."

"Just the same..."

He was interrupted by a ragged, black-bearded man who stepped casually from concealment. He wore a long tunic which divided into two parts from the belt downward. His bony ankles showed just above dusty, worn sandals. This was the costume of the Jewish laboring class. He wasn't a Sicarius, for he was armed with a heavy Roman javelin, or *pilum*. He'd probably stolen it and was a bandit. The Judean hills were full of them. Or, the youth decided, the man might be a Zealot, one of the fanatics who were recently rumored to have had enough of Roman rule. There had been Jews zealous for the Lord since the census rebellion of more than a half-century before. But these new type Zealots believed to be organizing were different. They were said to be planning to openly challenge the Romans who had occupied the land by military force for a hundred years.

The stranger leveled his weapon casually in the boys' direction. "Well, well! What have we here? Two young boys without the sense to travel with others?"

The man's voice was mocking, slow, but loaded with menace. The words seemed slightly slurred, perhaps from the scar, which made a white, twisted slash from the corner of his thin mouth across the right cheek toward the ear. The ear tip was missing.

"We're carrying this firewood to Jerusalem," the older youth said with rehearsed carefulness. "As you can see, we have nothing worth robbing."

"We shall see," the man with the spear said softly. He raised the metal weapon briefly above his head and lowered the butt to the rocky road. Two similarly dressed men appeared swiftly from the boulders. They produced short daggers, which the Romans called *sicarii*, and were synonymous with the assassins who killed soldiers or very Hellenized Jews in crowds and then vanished in the excitement. But the use of the daggers didn't necessarily mean the two newcomers were themselves Sicarii, the older youth told himself.

His younger companion came carefully around the donkey's hindquarters and stood close to his friend, as the two other men began poking at the load of firewood with the daggers. Both boys watched the glistening blades, until they were returned to the searchers' girdles.

The youths exchanged short, relieved glances, but their captors weren't through. Methodically, they began loosening the cracked leather fastenings and throwing the wood beside the roadway.

Triumphantly, the man on the animal's left side shoved the two lengths of wood aside and slid the parchment into full view.

"Ah!" The first man's exclamation wasn't slurred by his terrible scar. "What have we here?"

The youths met each other's eyes briefly. The older one sucked in his breath. "We don't know. It was given us to deliver."

The leader accepted the leather scroll and studied it thoughtfully. "What does it say?"

"We don't know," the youths said together.

The leader again raised his spear. A fourth man stood in the rocks. The youths saw at once he was a Gentile slave. He was slightly lighter colored than his companions, and only a stubble showed on his cheeks. He was used to being clean-shaven. He stepped into full view. The slave's collar was prominent, with the wide identification tag at the bottom of the collar, reflecting the sun.

"Read it," the leader ordered, handing over the scroll.

Silently, the slave obeyed. The youths saw that he was accustomed to handling such scrolls. They wondered why his slave collar hadn't been removed, if he had joined a bandit gang. Perhaps he was an unwilling member, or only recently escaped.

"Well?"

The slave cleared his throat. "It is written in Greek."

"You're a Greek! Read it."

The youths shifted uneasily, their dusty sandal soles feeling the sharp rocks in the road. The leader's dark eyes glistened with anticipation above the curling black beard. The scarred mouth curled into a crooked grin. Obviously, he thought something important had been inscribed on the leather scroll.

The slave said, "It seems to be addressed to a certain Theophilus."

The leader moved the Roman *pilum*. "Who's he?"

The leader tilted his spear, so the point rested lightly on the older youth's throat.

"Shall I ask again?"

The younger youth stepped forward and gently pushed the javelin point upward and away from his companion's throat. "He doesn't know, and neither do I."

"Don't tell me you two can't read?"

The leader's mocking words were again slurred by the scar. The older boy, emboldened by his friend's action with the spear, had his own fears calmed.

"We have learned because our fathers taught us," the older youth said with some pride, "but we have not read the words on that parchment."

"Why not?" the leader demanded.

"It was given us by . . . by one of those who follow The Way."

The leader's black eyes narrowed. "I have heard of them," he said softly. "They have such strange stories told about them. Is it true what is said?"

"I don't know," the older youth answered. "We are just delivering the scroll to a synagogue in the city."

The leader motioned with the spear. "Let's get out of this sun." He led the way through a narrow cleft in the rocks, toward the shadow of a cliff hill. It showed extensive layers of folded, reddish sediment from an age far beyond the memory of any man. The slave stood while the others sat against the cool cliffside. The man who'd found the scroll held the donkey's rope.

"Read it," the leader said again. "Let's find out who this Theophilus is."

The slave's identification label rose as the Gentile drew in a breath. "I have glanced at the words," he began, "and I don't see that this Theophilus is identified. A quick reading suggests that this is about some events which happened to your people."

"The Jews?"

The slave nodded. "Yes, but the writer doesn't seem to be one of yours."

"A Gentile?"

"Perhaps. The wording is such..."

"Just read it, then! After that, we'll decide what to do with these two young and foolish travelers."

The youths stood close together, feeling some measure of comfort in the pressure of their thin shoulders.

The other two bandits leaned forward eagerly. Perhaps the document contained information which might be useful to them.

The slave held the scroll before him and began to read aloud.

> Dear Theophilus:
>
> Many people have done their best to write a report of the things that have taken place among us. They wrote what we have been told by those who saw these things from the beginning and who proclaimed the message. And so, Your Excellency, because I have carefully studied all these matters from their beginning, I thought it would be good to write an orderly account for you. I do this so that you will know the full truth about everything which you have been taught.

The slave paused, glancing at the scarred leader.

The leader turned to the two youths. "What's he talking about in that parchment?"

The boys shook their heads and repeated they had not read the scroll. Their captor grunted and waved an impatient hand to the slave.

"Get on with it! Get to the meaning of the scroll."

"I believe that's next," the Gentile said politely.

"Then let's hear it." The leader jammed the butt end of the spear emphatically into the ground. "Let's hear it so we can decide what to do."

The slave cleared his throat again and read well: "During the time when Herod, king of Judea . . ."

"That tyrant!" The leader's scarred mouth twisted, opened wide, and a roar erupted from his bearded face. He leaped to his feet and snatched at the scroll. "It's because of the Herods that I hide in these rocks like a jackal! Do you boys know what Herod the king—that enemy of God and man—did to our nation; and what his sons have done? Do you?"

The older youth watched the parchment with concern, as the leader waved it emphatically in his left hand, while thrusting angrily at the sky with the spear.

"We know."

The other men were silent in the threat of the leader's intense anger.

The slave, however, seemed to have a look of doubt. "Herod the king has been dead several decades," the Gentile said uncertainly.

The leader threw the parchment onto the ground near the older youth's sandals. "Dead, yes! But his evil lives after him! His sons still live! The Rome he helped conquer us still lives! The Roman army of occupation still has us by the throat! Right here in our own homeland; the land the God of our fathers promised to Abraham and us forever! Until the last stench of the Herods is gone from this land, and the Romans with them, we shall never have that promise fulfilled! But it will come! It will come, I tell you!"

The patriotic fervor caused both youths to glance at each other with instant understanding. The younger whispered, "He's a Zealot."

The leader caught the word. "A Zealot? Yes, and proud of it! Don't whisper the word! Say it with pride! Do you know what a Zealot is, boy?"

The younger youth nodded, unsure of his voice in the explosive anger of the scar-faced leader.

"Then tell our Gentile friend here," the leader commanded, jerking his bearded chin toward the slave. "By the looks of his face, he hasn't been long enough in our land to know the truths which have torn our land and our people apart. Tell him!"

"Well," the younger youth said tentatively, "About two years after Herod the king died, a Jewish revolt began over a Roman census. The people involved were said to be zealous for the Lord, as our Scriptures teach us we should be. The term *Zealot* is not new. It simply means one who is a devout, unswerving monotheist. But there was no Zealot Party until recently. Now the movement has grown strong enough to openly threaten Rome in Jerusalem."

The youth stopped, wondering if he should say what he'd heard about the possibility that the Zealots might soon have an insurrection against the conquerors; that he'd heard there was a possibility the Temple would be destroyed in the fighting, especially if the Roman general, Vespasian, or his son, Titus, were to lead the counterattacks sure to come. The youth had decided not to mention the rising state of anxieties when the bandit's voice interrupted.

"Who started the party?" The leader's voice was lowering again, softening and slurring, as he regained control of his intense emotions.

"My friend here knows it better."

"Then let him tell it, and you listen well!"

The leader's eyes probed into the older youth's. He rubbed his hand uncertainly across the beginning beard and recited quickly and well.

"Pompey, the Roman general, took Jerusalem with the aid of the Idumean, Antipater, who was father to the tyrant, Herod. Herod the king was born about the time of Pompey's taking Jerusalem. In time, Caesar Augustus gave Herod the title, 'King of the Jews.'"

The Zealot leader snorted. "King of the Jews! He didn't have a drop of Jewish blood in him! Son of an Arabian and an Idumean, lover of Greek architecture and learning, Herod filled our land with his strange foreign buildings and ideas! He..."

The Zealot caught himself, took a deep breath, and motioned the young Jew to continue his recitation.

"Herod was deathly afraid of being supplanted on the throne. He had his favorite wife murdered, plus his brother-in-law, his mother-in-law..."

"And three of his own sons! Don't forget that! The third one just five days before the old tyrant died. But death did not free us of the Herods' tyranny! His eighteen-year-old son, Archelaus, succeeded him on the throne. And what did he do, my young friend?"

"Following the death of his father, Archelaus ordered his troops to subdue a crowd he thought was being unruly. This was at the Passover. So, when our people, the Jews, were offering their sacrifices, Archelaus's foot soldiers killed three thousand. At the Feast of Pentecost, barely forty days later, when Archelaus had gone to Rome to seek the emperor's confirmation of the late king's will, the Roman in charge, Quintilius Varus, crucified three thousand Jews."

"And that was just the beginning!" The Zealot leader waved the spear angrily. "There were other Jewish deaths, even though Archelaus reigned only half-a-dozen years. Then he was replaced by Roman procurators. They were a bad bunch, with Pontius Pilate the worst of the lot."

The Gentile slave cleared his throat. "I have seen that name in this scroll," he said.

The Zealot took a couple quick steps to the scroll, which the older Jewish boy had carefully picked up and rerolled. The Zealot seized the parchment and thrust it toward the slave with instructions to find the place. The leader turned to the older youth and urged him to continue his recitation.

"Well," he said, glancing thoughtfully at the sky, "the procurators ruled here in Judea, but Herod the king's son, Antipas, or Herod the Tetrach, governed the tetrachy in Galilee."

The leader nodded but made an impatient movement with the spear. "How about the Zealots? Tell our Gentile friend about us."

"Some people think the Zealots were formed when Judah the Galilean joined with Zadok the priest two years after Herod the king died, but actually that was only a short rebellion, which the Romans squashed. It started over a Roman census; the Jewish leaders thought we owed allegiance to no one but God; that paying taxes (which would have come as a result of the census) to the Romans was wrong. But actually, these resistance fighters were only zealous for the Lord, and the Zealot Party has only recently been said to exist. In fact, some people aren't even sure that it does exist formally. But this group and the one called by the same name when Judah the Galilean. . . ."

The leader interrupted with a sudden movement. He spun toward the youth. "Did you know that Judah was the son of Hezekiah, the one Herod the king killed before Herod really had gained full control of Jerusalem? And that Hezekiah's grandsons—Judah's sons—all three of them—carry on the cause this very hour? Did you know that Judah the Galilean was killed, because he opposed the census Quirinus conducted in Judea? Did you know that?"

The older youth nodded. "Judah believed that Roman rule was unlawful. He said that Israel owed allegiance only to God."

"Right! Right! You know your people's history well! The first people were zealous for the Lord, but the present Zealots are not the same as those who started under Judah the Galilean. And our cause today will not be so easily crushed by the Romans! We are stronger and wiser. Someday we'll control Jerusalem again. The Romans will be gone, and we patriots will again rule our own land, under God—blessed be His Name—just as He promised Abraham."

"When Messiah comes," one of the other Zealots said fervently.

The others all looked at the speaker. His eyes glistened with a softness, which startled the young captives.

The two boys were feeling better now that they knew they had not fallen into the hands of a dagger-wielding Sicarius but a Zealot or one who considered himself a member of that party. The leader didn't seem likely to harm two Jewish boys, although he might yet confiscate the precious scroll they'd been entrusted to carry to Jerusalem.

"Messiah," the Gentile said, breaking the boy's thoughts. "That word is in this scroll. I've been reading a little as you talked . . ." the Gentile said, "and I see that this scroll is about someone who is disputed as to whether or not he really was the Messiah."

"False Messiahs," the bandit leader said with a sigh. "How many of them there have been since the taste of freedom has been so long denied us! But someday . . ." He let his voice trail off.

The older youth asked, "But how shall we know when Messiah comes? I mean, with so many men claiming to be the Messiah these last few years?"

The bandit's scarred mouth moved. "You are fortunate to have a father who can read and write in a

land where most men—and no women—can do either.
You no doubt have read the Scriptures. What do they
say about the Messiah?"

The youth was thoughtful. There were three
possibilities, he had often heard: a Messiah like Moses,
one like David, or one like Zadok of the priestly line.
The youth wanted to get on toward Jerusalem with the
scroll, but he didn't want to antagonize the excitable
leader, who still held the two youths captive.

"It is written," the older boy began, "of the time
when Moses was talking to our ancestors. . . ."

The scarred leader interrupted. "Can you quote the
words from Moses?"

The youth nodded. "The Lord had been talking to
Moses about the time at Mount Sinai when the people
were afraid to see God's fiery presence any more for
fear they would die. Moses told the people, 'He will
send you a prophet like me from your own people, and
you are to obey him.'"

The boys' captor sighed and shook his head. "Such a
long time ago! How long before Messiah comes, I
wonder?"

The older youth decided not to mention the belief
that some Jews had of Messiah coming from the House
of David, while others expected a priestly Messiah, like
Zadok, who had been alive in the time of David and
Solomon. Later, Ezekiel had considered the only
legitimate priests were sons of Zadok. But mostly, the
youth thought, it was agreed the Messiah would be of
Davidic descent.

The youth said instead, "So many false Messiahs

have come forward in the last several years."

"But still you doubt the Messiah will come?"

The older youth shrugged. "I have heard about only one whom some say really *was* the Messiah...."

When the youth's sentence was left suspended and no one else spoke, the slave asked, "Shall I read on?"

The Zealot leader was thoughtful before he answered. "Read it," he announced finally. "And if there is nothing seditious in their scroll, we'll return it to these two and let them go. After all," he said with the twisted grin, "they may yet see things from the Zealot's viewpoint. And someday, when we take Jerusalem and drive out the Romans from our land, these youths may fight alongside us."

The three Zealots made themselves comfortable against the shady cliffside. The slave found his place and began reading.

During the time when Herod was king of Judea, there was a priest named Zechariah, who belonged to the priestly order of Abijah. His wife's name was Elizabeth; she also belonged to a priestly family. They both lived good lives in God's sight and obeyed fully all the Lord's laws and commands. They had no children because Elizabeth could not have any, and she and Zechariah were both very old. One day Zechariah was doing his work as a priest in the Temple, taking his turn in the daily service. According to the custom followed by the priests, he was chosen by lot to burn incense on the altar. So he went into the Temple of the Lord.

CHAPTER TWO

ZECHARIAH STOOD in the priest's room, clad in his headdress, coat, and girdle. It was not so ornate as the high priest's garments, which Herod the king had once kept locked up. That had a blue band atop the miter, with a gold plate at the brow. On top of the shoulders were the onyx stones with the names of the twelve tribes of Israel on each of the separate stones.

But Zechariah, as one of the common priests, wore the less elaborate headdress, a plain coat, and narrow girdle. Zechariah, moving slowly because of his years, tied the bright sash about his middle to indicate he had been selected for duty that day. He brushed his full gray beard with stiffening fingers and reached for a small incense pot. He was ready.

Outside, activities in the various courtyards had begun. At the boundaries, covered walks with open colonnades on one side, called cloisters, were supported by marble Corinthian columns. Three men joining hands could scarcely reach around any of these multiple monoliths. Across from the cloisters was the open Court of the Gentiles and the Temple proper beyond that. In the outer, open area were the money-changers' booths, stalls for sacrificial animals awaiting sale, and porticoes or rooms where students met with teachers. This outer area had wide steps to an inner Court of the Women, which was also open to men who came with their wives, but was forbidden to non-Jews.

A second flight of steps led through gold and silver plated gates to the Court of the Priests. The sacrificial altar was here, in the open air. But Zechariah's goal was beyond this, up more steps to bronze doors seventy-five feet high and twenty-four feet wide. This was the entrance to the Temple proper. The structure was of white marble with a gold-plated facade. Inside, Zechariah would enter the second most sacred spot, the Holy Place. Beyond it, separated by two veils hung nearly two feet apart, was the Holy of Holies into which only the high priest could enter, and that just once yearly.

Jews considered the Temple at Jerusalem the most beautiful building in the world. Herod the king had begun building it about a dozen years before. At first, the Jews had been suspicious, for Herod wanted to replace the insignificant remains of Zerubbabel's five-hundred-year-old Temple with something more like the original splendor, which had been Solomon's Temple. It had been the first to stand upon this sacred mountain in Jerusalem.

The Temple area was perched in majestic splendor upon Mount Moriah, where Abraham was believed to have offered Isaac centuries before. The city was nearly impregnable from attack, with the deep Kidron Valley separating it from the Mount of Olives on the east, the Tyropoean Valley on the west, a moat to the north, and still another valley to the south.

The Jews hadn't wanted Herod the king to tear down Zerubbabel's Temple, but the monarch had prevailed, as he always did. He had not betrayed the Jews, but instead, in his passion for building, had erected the most magnificent structure in anyone's memory. Although the New Temple still wasn't finished, as Zechariah prepared for his morning duty, it was such a tremendous undertaking that it would be worth waiting for many more years.

The new Temple graced thirty-five acres of Jerusalem with white stone. This native product, cut and polished, glistened so that the sun rising over the Mount of Olives was reflected back with a glory which sucked men's breath from them in astonishment.

Zechariah left the priest's robing room and entered the middle area called Court of the Israelites, where men had gathered for the service. Zechariah made his way on to the Court of the Priests. This area was forbidden to all except the priests. The aged Zechariah moved slowly across this toward the immense gates of the Temple itself.

Zechariah was one of about eighteen thousand ordinary priests in one of the twenty-four divisions. Most of the year, Zechariah lived at home like the other priests. But this was the week Zechariah had been chosen by lot to offer incense in the Holy Place.

A ceremonious escort of four Temple priests, similarily clad except for the bright sash, followed Zechariah through the priests' courtyard. Two of the accompanying priests carried the loaves of shewbread. These twelve fine white flour loaves were to be laid in two rows on the inner shrine's table of gold. They would be placed on spice-filled chalices. The loaves would stay there until the following Sabbath, when fresh ones would be brought and the old ones divided among the priests. A third priest carried a pan-shaped incense brazier. The fourth accompanying priest's hands were free to open the smaller door in the great entrance to the Holy Place.

Zechariah moved slowly, feeling his age. His eyes raised to the sanctuary doorway. Eight heraldic trumpeters flanked the door where Zechariah stopped. His four companion priests entered the sanctuary, but Zechariah turned and led the nonattending priests in an ancient chorus of words:

"May the God of mercy enter the sanctuary, and may He be pleased to accept the sacrifice of His people."

The four priests returned empty-handed to the courtyard. Zechariah turned and slowly entered alone into the sanctuary or Holy Place.

He stood for a moment, letting his eyes accustom themselves to the startlingly dark room, which was adjacent to that most unusual place of worship in all the world.

Unbelievers like Pompey, the Roman conqueror of

Jerusalem, had profaned the most sacred spot by entering it about half a century ago. He had not plundered the place, but his blasphemous act had shocked the Jews. To the unbelievers like Pompey, it was unthinkable that not a thing resembling an idol was harbored there. The Jews and their invisible God were united in an unseen bond which only the Jews seemed to comprehend.

But Zechariah, standing in the vaulted, dark room, was filled with the sense of God's Presence. The room was so large that walls and ceilings were indiscernible. The impact was awesome. The only light was from a massive gold menorah ten-feet high. The seven branches held the flickering flames of light, which allowed the old priest to finally make out the other three dominant features.

The blue, finely woven veil separated the priest from the sacrosanct Holy of Holies beyond. Nearer to Zechariah, the Altar of the Incense, with its brazier of living coals, and the waist-high table of shewbread slowly evolved into recognizable objects.

Still not moving, so that his old eyes could make their slow adjustment, Zechariah glanced again at the veil which separated mortal men from the Presence beyond.

Outside, the first flourish of trumpets gave Zechariah his cue. He approached the altar with the box of incense. Slowly he sprinkled its contents onto the brazier. Thick smoke arose toward the dark, unseen ceiling. Slowly, reverently, the priest bowed his head to pray.

Outside, in the daylight of a new morning, the worshipers saw a column of smoke curl upward from the sanctuary roof. The trumpeters lowered their instruments. Worship had started.

In the soft darkness of the sanctuary, Zechariah bent his body in front of the altar and intoned, "May the God of mercy enter the sanctuary and be pleased to accept the sacrifice of His people."

Zechariah closed his eyes momentarily against the effects of the burning incense. When he opened them again, he blinked in surprise and he stepped back in alarm. Through the diffused smoke rising from the altar, Zechariah saw the figure of what appeared at first glance to be a man. The old priest's bearded face contorted in fear. No one was supposed to be in here!

Zechariah stared hard at the unexpected visitor. He was radiant in a way no mortal had ever been. Zechariah glimpsed a young man of such intense brightness that the old priest stumbled backward. He instinctively covered his eyes with withered hands. Yet, even in that second, Zechariah knew he had seen the almost-beautiful countenance of the Lord's angel.

"Don't be afraid, Zechariah!"

The words, soft and melodious as a Judean spring waterfall, caused the old priest to cautiously open his fingers and peer between them.

The angel's quiet voice continued. "God has heard your prayer and your wife Elizabeth will bear you a son."

Weak-kneed, Zechariah carefully, cautiously dropped his hands. The fluttering light flames from the gold menorah and the coals from the brazier showed the gentleness of the speaker's countenance.

"You are to name him," the angel said after a slight pause, "John."

Still, the priest did not speak. He stared in fascination through the incense smoking from the altar, as the angel spoke again.

"How glad and happy you will be, and how happy many others will be when he is born! He will be a great man in the Lord's sight."

Zechariah blinked hard, but the figure before him was still there, still speaking.

"From his very birth, he will be filled with the Holy Spirit, and he will bring back many of the people of Israel to the Lord their God. He will go ahead of the Lord, strong and mighty like the prophet Elijah. He will bring fathers and children together again; he will turn disobedient people back to the way of thinking of the righteous; he will get the Lord's people ready for him."

Zechariah, overwhelmed, but feeling his fear receding, found his voice. "How shall I know if this is so? I am an old man, and my wife is old also."

"I am Gabriel." The simple pronouncement hung in the great vaulted room with powerful overtones. "I stand in the presence of God, who sent me to speak to you and tell you this good news."

The angel's voice changed slightly in mild reproach. "But you have not believed my message, which will come true at the right time. Because you have not believed, you will be unable to speak; you will remain silent until the day my promise to you comes true."

The worshipers in the Temple courtyard stirred uneasily. They raised their eyes thoughtfully to the silent, closed sanctuary door. Men turned carefully to each other and whispered, "What's keeping Zechariah so long?"

Zechariah stumbled out of the darkened room and into the priests' court. He crossed it with unsteady steps and re-entered the Court of Israel. The men shifted uncertainly as the old priest's lips moved, but no sounds came. The gray beard shook. His tongue vainly tried to form words, then rested across his lower lip, protruding out of his open mouth. He began making gestures with his pale hands, but he was totally mute. However, the men got the idea: Zechariah had seen a vision.

Several miles away and some time later, a young woman named Mary was washing laundry at a stream outside Nazareth. Behind her, the Galilean town snuggled comfortably into the verdant hills.

Mary was very young, beautiful, and strong. She raised her dark eyes and smiled at some goats grazing in the distance. Her black hair was barely visible over her wide, smooth forehead. A plain white scarf spilled down over her ears, allowing only the lobes to show. Her lithe form was covered with a sleeved tunic much like Jewish men wore. Since it was summer, Mary wore this undergarment next to her olive colored skin. It fell to her ankles and was seamless. She had stitched it together from two rectangular sheets, each two-and-a-half feet long along the narrow edge. A hole had been left for her head. The wool tunic was gathered at the waist by a light leather girdle. In the winter, she would have worn a cloak as an outer garment, called the mantle.

Mary bent over the stream to rinse her wash. A man's reflection was momentarily caught in the stream, then washed away with the current. But Mary didn't notice.

She straightened up and turned toward a large flat rock. She glanced casually around. No one was in sight. Mary laid the wet wash on the rock and began the age-old beating process.

Mary was happy. She had entered into a betrothal to Joseph, a descendant of the great King David, whose son, Solomon, had built the first Temple at Jerusalem nearly a thousand years before. The betrothal of Joseph and Mary was part of the two-step-marriage arrangement, which was part of the ancient Jewish tradition. In time, the couple would be married, as the second step in the Jewish custom.

There were some who thought this a bad time to be married and bring children into the world. Galilee to the north and Judah to the south, with the Samaritan populace between, groaned under the Roman occupation forces. Not that the Jews were much used to freedom; except for a short period under the Maccabees, after the Greeks had occupied the land, the Jews hadn't governed themselves in centuries.

There were no schools for Jewish children, but Mary had heard about her people and their God since she was a child. She might not have known the Scriptures, from attending the synagogue, but she certainly knew the background of her people. Such learning came through the father, who had heard it from his father before him.

In every Jewish home, hope for the Messiah's coming was high.

That expectation had been rising for many years. It had risen and fallen with the peoples' troubles from other nations.

Saul had been Israel's first king. He had united the northern tribes of Israel and the southern ones of Judah. The famous King David had succeeded him. His son, Solomon, had erected the first Temple where Herod's was still being built.

There had been civil war under Solomon's son, and the kingdom had again been divided into north and south.

The Assyrians, an ancient Mesopotamian kingdom, had conquerered the northern kingdom some seven hundred years before. In their customary manner, the victors deported prisoners from their homeland to Assyria. This happened to the northern tribes and then in Samaria. Sargon II claimed he deported only twenty-seven thousand persons, so most of the descendants of Ephraim and Manasseh never left their homes in Samaria.

About a century-and-a-half later, the Babylonians exiled the remaining tribes from the south, so Judah was depopulated. The Persians who succeeded the Babylonians allowed the Jews a large measure of self-government. But some of the Jews returned to Jerusalem, rebuilt the wall and a smaller version of the Temple, called Zerubbabel's. It had stood until a few years before, when Herod the king began erecting the magnificent new one called Second Temple.

The people had never been long without troubles, however. The Macedonian-speaking Greeks under Alexander the Great had conquered the Jews' homeland and introduced Hellenism four hundred years before.

When Alexander died, his generals warred among themselves, with their descendants, called Ptolemies and Seleucids, had ruled Palestine. These people spoke Greek and were called *Seleucids* in Syria to the northeast and *Ptolemies* in Egypt. Sometimes the Seleucids could be called *Syrian-Greeks* and the Ptolemies, *Egyptian Greeks.* Although the Jews generally were hopelessly Hellenized, and Greek was spoken in Palestine, Aramaic was spoken by most Jews.

There had been a period of self-rule by the Jews after the Maccabees had overthrown the Syrian-born Antiochus IV (Epiphanes), who had outraged the Jews by sacrificing a swine on their sacred altar about a hundred and sixty years before.

But the descendants of the Maccabees had quarrelled, and the Romans under Pompey had seized Jerusalem more than half a century before. Since then, Mary knew, the Romans had ruled the land. The Jews had been under a foreign occupation army, usually not too visible, but present, nevertheless. Herod the king now ruled by right of the Roman emperor, but Herod was now getting old. His terrible temper and fear of losing the throne were worse than ever. He had killed countless people, including his own favorite wife and two of their sons. A third son was said to be imprisoned at that moment, while the king made up his mind whether to have him strangled, too, as a contender for the throne.

Mary wondered, with all her people, would it ever end before Messiah came? And when would he come? There was no doubt he would; the question was: when?

In the Greek language, the Hebrew word *Messiah* was rendered as Christ. Either way, as *Messiah* in Hebrew or *Christ* in Greek, the word meant "anointed one." The sacred writings were full of promises: God would visit His chosen people, and they would have their Messiah.

The messianic hope was high in the land, for Herod the king was brutal beyond words. He held the title of King of the Jews by authority of the Roman emperor, and the Romans controlled much of the world. Galilee and Judea were small portions of the sprawling Roman empire. Herod was an Idumean, born in the ancient land of Esau or Edom to the south of Judea. Once the Idumeans had been forcibly converted to Judaism, a contrary practice to the peaceful followers of the invisible God.

Since Herod ruled well from Rome's viewpoint, he held the title and the power; the Jews, captives in their own land, waited for the Messiah.

But when would Messiah come?

Mary was alone in a small white-washed room folding the now-dry laundry, when she became conscious of being watched. She paused in her work, cut her eyes quickly to the right, then the left. She sucked in her breath and looked up.

Gabriel, radiant as he had been six months before

when he spoke to the priest in the sanctuary, stood before Mary.

She was only a little startled. There was none of the alarm in her which Zechariah had experienced.

Gabriel's soft, pleasant voice reassured Mary. "Peace be with you!" he said in the traditional Jewish greeting.

Mary nodded uncertainly.

Gabriel continued, "The Lord is with you and has greatly blessed you!"

Mary swallowed slowly, saying nothing; but she was troubled.

"Don't be afraid, Mary; God has been gracious to you."

Mary was surprised to hear her name.

Gabriel said, "You will become pregnant and give birth to a son, and you will name him Jesus."

Embarrassed, Mary looked away.

Gabriel's reassuring tones came to her again. "He will be great and will be called The Son of the Most High God.

"The Lord God will make him a king, as his ancestor David was, and he will be the king of the descendants of Jacob forever; his kingdom will never end!"

Mary said boldly, "I am a virgin. How, then, can this be?"

"The Holy Spirit will come on you, and God's power will rest upon you. For this reason the holy child will be called the Son of God."

Mary listened silently as the angel explained that her relative Elizabeth was now six months pregnant. Even though she was very old, and it was said she couldn't have children, she was going to have a baby.

The angel paused, looked deeply into Mary's brown eyes and said, "For there is nothing that God cannot do."

Mary nodded slowly and lowered her eyes. "I am the Lord's servant. May it happen to me as you have said."

When Mary raised her eyes, the angel was gone.

Mary was alone, thinking what it all meant.

CHAPTER THREE

MARY RODE A DONKEY through the hill country of Judea toward the home of Elizabeth and Zechariah. As Mary watched the small boy leading her animal along a stony path, the angel's words echoed in Mary's mind.

Mary's attention was jerked abruptly to the present. She heard the sound of some boisterous men who were approaching. Mary looked anxiously toward the yet-unseen men. Herodian soldiers, perhaps? No. They were disciplined. King Herod himself was a madman, but he insisted his troops be discreet and restrained. Although they were garrisoned in Palestine, the soldiers were usually kept out of sight. Bandits? Mary gave an involuntary shudder. The mountains were full of bandits, and had been for generations. Herod, as a young man, had made a great effort to stamp them out, but the Judean hills were full of limestone caves and other places an outlaw might hide.

Mary motioned to the boy leading her donkey. The boy nodded and led the animal off the path. It was understandable about the bandits: Jew or Gentile, they represented the poorest of the poor. Almost everyone, it seemed, was poor in Palestine. But the outlaws, excluded from the normal economics for various reasons, turned on society and preyed on anyone they could.

The little donkey followed the lead boy and stood quietly behind a rocky outcropping. The relentless sun beat down on the animal and the two people. Mary watched the approaching bandits with anxious eyes. The road journey was long, but would be longer, if these men saw her. They passed without seeing the girl and her mount. When their laughter had died out, she nodded to the boy. Wordlessly, he led the small-footed donkey back onto the road. The journey continued.

Zechariah sat in his home in the Judean hills with a quill pen and parchment. His split-reed pen had been introduced by Greek scribes more than two centuries before. Most men still used a rush with frayed end as a kind of small brush to write on leather or papyrus. But Zechariah was ahead of his time, using the quill to copy Torah on parchment.

He sat on a stool with four slender wood legs and a leather seat stretched taut. His work lay on a low wooden table of equal simplicity.

The old priest looked up with a smile, as his wife entered. She bore the midday meal of cheese and goat's milk. Her pregnancy was showing.

Elizabeth took her husband's quill from his hand and

placed the pen on the table. She guided his hand and tenderly placed it against her abdomen.

"Now at last," she said softly, "the Lord has helped me. He has taken away my disgrace."

Her husband smiled. A loving, light, playful attitude was momentarily displayed between the couple. Then Zechariah lifted his bearded face and his lips parted in a proud smile.

The couple stopped suddenly, cocking their heads. "Did you hear something?" Elizabeth asked.

Outside the simple home, the boy dropped the donkey's lead rope. Mary urged it into a trot the last fifty yards to the priest's house. Mary slid quickly to the ground and ran to the open doorway.

"Elizabeth?"

The contrast of the darkened interior against the brilliant sunlight momentarily blinded Mary. She shaded her eyes and peered through the open door.

"Elizabeth?" she called again.

The priest's wife came as quickly as her condition permitted. She opened her arms wide and cried, "Cousin Mary!"

The women embraced fondly with happy exclamations.

"Uh!" Elizabeth let out a short, sharp gasp. She put her hand over her distended abdomen.

"The baby just kicked," she explained with a broad grin.

Mary stepped back and looked happily at Elizabeth. Mary's eyes turned down at her own trim figure. Slowly, tentatively, Mary knelt. She placed her young firm fingers gently on Elizabeth's abdomen. Impulsively, Mary nestled her face there.

The old priest's wife glowed with a mysterious light.
The Holy Spirit was upon her.

She said softly, quietly, "You are the most blessed of
all women, and blessed is the child you will bear!"

Mary didn't seem surprised that her cousin already
knew about the early pregnancy. Mary rose from her
knees, as Elizabeth's hands tugged tenderly at Mary's
smooth hands. There was awe in the older woman's
voice as she spoke again.

"Why should this great thing happen to me, that my
Lord's mother comes to visit me? For as soon as I heard
your greeting, the baby within me jumped with
gladness."

That night, Mary spread a cloth on the table and
helped set out food. Zechariah lighted the oil lamps.
Mary moved slowly past him and stood thoughtfully
gazing out the small window.

"My heart praises the Lord," Mary began. Her voice
was barely audible in the happy house. "My soul is glad
because of God my Savior, for He has remembered me,
his lowly servant!"

Mary turned, facing the old couple who stood in rapt
silence. Mary continued, "From now on, all people will
call me happy, because of the great things the Mighty
God has done for me."

The younger woman lifted her hands. "His name is
holy; from one generation to another he shows mercy to
those who honor him.

"He has stretched out his mighty arm and scattered
the proud with all their plans."

Mary lowered her eyes. "He has brought down mighty kings from their thrones, and lifted up the lowly.

"He has filled the hungry with good things, and sent the rich away with empty hands."

The young woman's eyes were moist in the light of the oil lamp as she raised her face toward the old couple. Mary continued her soliloquy:

"He has kept the promise he made to our ancestors, and has come to the help of his servant Israel.

"He has remembered to show mercy to Abraham and to all his descendants forever!"

Three months later, the same room was filled with joyful neighbors. Elizabeth's figure was trim. Her proud husband, still mute, stood somberly at her side. Their eyes were on an elderly man holding their baby boy. The Mohel moved forward and raised his circumcision knife.

There was a sharp cry from the infant. His cries were immediately drowned in a chorus of adult rejoicing. A totally gray-bearded neighbor reached for Zechariah's hand, looked at the boy and pronounced a new name: "Zechariah!"

Elizabeth raised her hands.

"No!" she exclaimed. "His name is to be John."

Another neighbor laid a restraining hand on the new mother's shoulder. "But you don't have any relative with that name!"

Zechariah's mouth moved but he could not speak. For nine months, his tongue had been silent. Now,

nodding vehemently, he reached to his study table. All
the rejoicing neighbors subsided into watchful silence,
as the old priest picked up a stylus and quickly brushed
parchments aside, until he found a blank wax tablet.

Painfully, his old fingers grasping the stylus,
Zechariah formed Hebrew characters. The elderly
neighbor peered over the priest's shoulder and read, as
each character was formed:

"His . . . name . . . is . . . John!"

"John? John!" the chorus turned from questioning
inflections of surprise and doubt to emphatic acceptance: "His name is John!"

The new father's hands shook. He dropped the
stylus. Every eye focused on him. His mouth worked
under the gray beard, as he tried to break the months of
silence.

"Blessed . . ." Zechariah said with difficulty, and then
with soaring joy, "Blessed . . . be . . . the Lord!"

He fell on his knees. His arms were raised in ecstasy.

The neighbors clustered about him, as tears formed
in the old priest's dark eyes. His chin quivered but his
newly found voice was strong.

"Let us praise the Lord, the God of Israel! He has
come to the help of his people and has set them free!"

Slowly, with dignity, and yet motivated by a
powerful inner strength, Zechariah rose. "He has
provided for us a mighty Savior; a descendant of his
servant David. He promised through his holy prophets
long ago that he would save us from our enemies, from
the power of all those who hate us. . . ."

As if to shout his message to the world, Zechariah

moved toward the open door. "He said he would show mercy to our ancestors and remember his sacred covenant. . . ."

Zechariah touched the mezuzah on the doorpost with his finger and then kissed the finger. The assembled neighbors remained politely silent as the old priest continued. "With a solemn oath to our ancestor Abraham he promised to rescue us from our enemies and allow us to serve him without fear, so that we might be holy and righteous before him all the days of our life."

Zechariah turned. Elizabeth was there with their son. Gently, the priest picked up the newly named John. He had stopped crying. Softly, quietly, Zechariah spoke to his son.

"You, my child, will be called a prophet of the Most High God. You will go ahead of the Lord to prepare his road for him, to tell his people that they will be saved by having their sins forgiven."

Zechariah's eyes left his son's face and sought the skies beyond the room's ceiling. "Our God is merciful and tender. He will cause the bright dawn of salvation to rise on us and to shine from heaven on all those who live in the dark shadow of death; to guide our steps into the path of peace."

For a moment, the neighbors were hushed, still caught up in the conviction of the old priest's words. Then some frowned, for it was a prophetic declaration from a knowledgeable priest of the Most High God, but there were very real dangers in Judea that day. Herod the king, who had killed his favorite wife and two of his

sons to protect the throne, would not yield to anyone—
prophet or prince—who sought to guide the Jews' steps
toward any peace Herod had not decreed.

A short time later, in the pretty little Nazareth
community north of Galilee, an official mounted the
synagogue steps. Two Roman soldiers flanked him
with legs widespread in a determined stance. Each
legionnaire wore a round iron helmet with decorative
crest, cheek pieces to the ears, and a hinged visor. They
wore bright red tunics and leather cuirass encompassed
their chests. The two rectangular shields, curved to
their bodies, and held in the left hands, partially hid the
shoulder pieces, which were wired to the corset. A heart
guard of plated bronze was worn under the two
shoulder pieces. Their uniforms fell to the knees,
bronze greaves covered the forepart of the legs from
knees to ankles.

But it was their Roman weapons which reminded the
Jews of Rome's unconquerable might. The soldier on
the right gripped the standard throwing spear in his
right hand. His short sword brushed the same elbow.
The second soldier also wore the sheathed sword, but in
his right hand was a wicked-looking two-edged ax.

The Jews wilted into silence. The Roman official
raised the rolled scroll, spread it expertly, and read in
stentorian tones.

"Know all men of Nazareth, that by command of
Caesar Augustus, there will be conducted a census of
Palestine, a province of Syria."

The crowd groaned collectively. The official's eyes

glittered warningly over the top of the scroll. Silence returned instantly. He continued.

"All men must register forthwith in the towns and cities of their ancestral birth."

The announcement signaled immediate hubbub with occasional loud shouts from the safety of the crowd's back rows.

The official ignored the protests. He turned briskly and emphatically nailed the proclamation to the synagogue door with his sword hilt.

The soldiers' faces remained hard and unmoved. The official's eyes swept the crowd, pausing now and then to mark an anguished cry.

"What do the Romans want from us?"

The soldiers' eyes shifted to an angry, young, bearded face, then slid off as another yelled, "Why can't they leave us alone?"

A woman, face tear-stained and weary, pushed her way through the men and called to the official. "My husband is sick! He can't make such a trip!"

The official stabbed her with cold, dark eyes. "No exceptions! Caesar has spoken!" He gave the scroll nail an emphatic blow with the sword hilt and deftly returned the ugly weapon to its scabbard.

The crowd groaned. The soldiers and the official stood, widelegged and challenging. The Jews knew thousands of their friends and neighbors had been crucified or marched off to slavery—sometimes a whole town at once—for opposing the might of Caesar's occupation forces.

Slowly, fighting back sobs of frustration and anger,

the crowd began to drift away. But one, more angry or daring than the others, shook his fist above his companions' heads and cried the thought that was in everyone's mind:

"Wait until Messiah comes!"

The official snorted. "You Jews have been looking for Messiah for centuries! He's not coming! And even if he did, what could he do against Imperial Rome?"

The question rang in the air, unanswered. But as the crowd dispersed, they looked at each other and nodded through their hurt and despair.

Messiah would come. The ancient prophets had promised that—over and over. He would come; hopefully, he would come soon.

Chapter Four

Mary was in her ninth month of pregnancy. Still, she walked beside a donkey which her husband, Joseph, led from Nazareth south out of Galilee, around despised Samaria and toward the Judean hills. But Mary could not walk all the way. She rested sometimes on the donkey, which also carried the couple's few belongings.

There were surprisingly few signs of the occupation army. The Roman garrisons in Palestine were small and usually kept out of sight. They could be counted on, however, to show up at the Passover and other Jewish celebrations, where large crowds would gather. The presence of troops then was meant to keep the peace by implied force.

Only once did the couple on their way to Bethlehem see any signs of the quiet efficiency by which Rome ruled this small land-bridge between Egypt and

Mesopotamia and other warlike peoples. A slave trader's convoy met them, heading north. About twenty-five Jewish men and women were strung together, as a public display of Roman might. Apparently, some officer had been displeased with a village and had carried the whole population off as slaves. It was a common-enough occurrence, but better than crucifixion.

The soldiers escorting the prisoners marched with the assuredness of the powerful, the invincible army, which had conquered everything from the island of Britain, far to the west, north to Gaul, south to Egypt and Africa, and east to the great river, the Euphrates.

Mary and Joseph exchanged sorrowful glances. Then she touched her swelling abdomen and smiled down from her seat on the burro's sturdy back. Joseph returned the smile and pulled more urgently on the lead rope.

They passed Jerusalem and continued south and slightly west another five miles or so. Night had settled before they reached Joseph's ancestral home.

Bethlehem was a small, unwalled town. It was best known as the City of David, named for the Jewish shepherd boy who had become king. Nearly a thousand years before, after Saul had died in battle, David had succeeded him as head of the unified monarchy. David had transformed it into an empire. Centuries before David, descendants of Abraham, Isaac, and Jacob had become a nation at Sinai, the mountain of God, after fleeing Egypt's four hundred and thirty years of bondage. But they had been twelve tribes—not one kingdom—before Saul became the Hebrews' first king.

Many centuries before that, God had promised the nomadic people's founding father, Abraham, a special land to be theirs forever. "I promise," God had said, "to give your descendants all this land from the border of Egypt to the Euphrates River...." At the time, Abraham didn't have any children, but the patriarch had believed God.

When Abraham died, a father and founder of nations, he had not owned much of the land promised him and his descendants forever. There had been the Machpelah Cave, which Abraham had bought from Ephron the Hittite for four hundred pieces of silver to bury his wife, Sarah. A well had been dug by Abraham and confirmed by Abimelech, who had given seven lambs as proof of ownership. The agreement was made at Beersheba. Abraham had owned only a tiny bit of land, but it was a start on the Promised Land.

However, the Hebrews were still a nation without any real area of the Promised Land when God visited them at Sinai in the peninsula desert far to the south of Bethlehem. Still, the Hebrews (as they were then known) had believed the promise of their invisible God. Moses had led them out of Egypt and to the edge of the Promised Land. Moses had died without entering it. His successor, Joshua, had led the Hebrews, as they penetrated the land of Canaan at Jericho. They and their descendants had gone on to conquer the whole Promised Land.

Joseph thought about the past and his own Davidic heritage. Recently he had faced a hard decision over

Mary's pregnancy. Should he "put her away," like an annulment of their betrothal before the second marriage step was taken? Assured by divine pronouncement that the child Mary carried was conceived miraculously and was of God, Joseph had decided. He would wed Mary when the betrothal period had been completed.

By then, Mary would have been delivered of her first-born child and they would name him Jesus, as instructed.

Joseph felt a rising concern, as he saw the teeming, narrow and dirty streets of his ancestral hometown. The emperor's census decree had flooded Bethlehem with far more travelers than there were lodging facilities. The inns were built in a square with a courtyard enclosed. The Nazarene couple entered the outer gate and halted in surprise. By the torches which flickered fitfully over the inn's courtyard walls, Joseph and Mary saw the milling throngs. There were angry shouts. Tempers were frayed. Vendors of food and drink hawked their wares, heedless of the human despair all around them.

Mary, still mounted, suddenly clutched her abdomen. Her young, pretty face blanched with the first labor pain.

Joseph caught the sign. He pushed his way through the crowd toward the beleaguered innkeeper. All about him angry voices cried out.

"They told us there was room at this inn!"

"Look what these thieves are charging for a piece of bread!"

"If the Romans want us to enroll, they ought to make sure there's a place to stay."

Joseph paid no heed. Spurred by necessity, he reached the innkeeper. He was a Jew, stocky and strong, with bare forearms.

Mary, unable to hear over the crowd noises, saw the innkeeper shake his head. Mary saw Joseph point to her and urgently tug at the innkeeper's sleeve. Mary saw the man's eyes open wide in understanding.

She guessed he was a father himself; certainly he was a compassionate man! Mary saw him seize a torch from a wall bracket, hold it high and push hard through the throng toward her.

Mary caught the urgency in crowd voices, "Sir! I need a. . . ." Mary missed the word, but she knew what he needed. Everyone needed a room when there was none.

The innkeeper shook off one man's desperate grip. "No more room! I'm full. You'll have to go somewhere else."

"But they sent me here!" the man's anguished voice penetrated through the crowd's babble. "They said you had space!"

"Are you deaf?" the innkeeper shouted angrily to the man. The innkeeper kept walking, holding up the torch while Joseph led the way.

Mary let out a sharp cry.

The innkeeper and Joseph were at her side. The innkeeper held the light high to look at Mary. "Come with me!" he ordered. "There's a place in back, where I stable the animals."

He led the way. Joseph steadied Mary on the donkey's back.

Mary bit her lower lip and sucked in her breath. There wasn't anyone in the noisy, unhappy crowd who didn't see Joseph and Mary's plight with a momentary thought: "At least I'm better off than they!"

The stable was typical of the area. One of the countless Judean limestone caves had been converted to practical use. A roof and three sides had already been provided before any animal was ever stabled there. The innkeeper had only to close the entrance, and he had an inexpensive and dependable area for his animals.

The innkeeper stuck the torch in a wall bracket above a rock ledge. "There," he said, turning around with a broad sweep of his hands, "It's clean. And it will have to do."

Joseph was overwhelmed. The poor of the land were grateful for what the Lord provided. Even for the birth of a child.

Joseph tried to make Mary comfortable on a bed of straw. The innkeeper hurried off, leaving his light behind. He called, "I'll see if I can find a midwife."

Mary's pains were coming closer together. Suddenly, she gasped and grabbed her abdomen. Joseph, alone in an ancient, tormented town where everyone was in some kind of anguish, looked anxiously at Mary.

Not far from Jerusalem, three shepherds were tending their flock. Only one was awake. He sat watchfully in a barren, rock-strewn field, playing a shepherd's pipe. His gaze touched his two sleeping

companions, slipped on through the starry night to
where the black-faced sheep huddled together. Most of
them seemed to be asleep also.

Suddenly, the sheep leaped to their feet as one. They
darted in a body to the right, swerved sharply left, and
then circled, bleating and shuffling nervously in a tight,
gray band of motion.

The shepherd shoved his pipe into his belt and stood
up quickly, crook gripped firmly to ward off the unseen
disturber.

The shepherd's eyes swept the darkness beyond the
sheep and then came to rest on a startling apparition.

The angel Gabriel, luminous as a thousand oil lamps,
materialized before the startled shepherd's wide eyes.

Terrified, the shepherd dropped his crook and threw
himself face down onto the ground. He lay there
beneath his cloak, shaking with fear, until he heard a
voice.

"Don't be afraid."

At first, the shepherd wasn't sure whether to believe
the melodious, assuring words. But as the shepherd
dared to peer cautiously from the earth, he saw the
gentle, quiet countenance of his visitor.

The other shepherds awakened. They rose to their
knees but fell prone again at the sight of Gabriel. The
first shepherd tried to form a question, but his tongue
clacked on a dry mouth.

The visitor spoke again, his words like rippling
sounds of spring water. "I am here with good news for
you, which will bring great joy to all the people."

All three shepherds shook with fear but felt a

growing assurance as the visitor looked benignly at each one by turn.

"This very day," Gabriel continued, "in David's town your Savior was born—Christ the Lord. And this is what will prove it to you: you will find a baby wrapped in cloths and lying in a manger."

The shepherd's eyes were swept upward as the heavens suddenly burst with myriads of new stars and a chorus of angelic voices swept all fear aside with glorious sounds of joy.

"Glory to God in the highest heaven," the angelic choir proclaimed to the shepherds. "Glory to God in the highest heaven, and peace on earth to those with whom he is pleased!"

The three shepherds' eyes, dazzled by the starry display, looked away from the lofty chorus in the sky to the place where Gabriel had stood. The angel was gone. The astonished shepherds looked at each other in disbelief. They were alone in the field.

For a moment, they looked at each other in speechless wonder. Then, as one, they left their sheep and turned their steps toward the little town of Bethlehem, glistening in the distance.

The midwife finished cleaning up and left. Mary lay exhausted in the cave-stable. Her face was wet with the hard labor she had experienced. Her dark hair fell in damp wisps. There was a smile of joy and fulfillment on her lips. She reached wearily to help Joseph finish wrapping the child in swaddling clothes.

As the newborn babe filled the tiny cave with the crying of new life, Joseph moved a donkey standing near its manger. He replaced the straw with fresh handfuls. He lifted the child from his mother's arms and gently laid him in the manger. Joseph stood looking down in wonder.

A voice asked plaintively, "Is the child here?"

Mary and Joseph were startled by the shepherd's voice. The couple turned to the cave entrance. The three shepherds stood awkwardly, uncertain of what to do.

Mary and Joseph exchanged bewildered glances. Then understanding passed between them. The couples' faces dissolved into smiles of further joy.

Joseph stepped forward, beckoning the visitors in out of the night. "He *is* here! And you are welcome!"

The shepherds followed Joseph to the manger. They gazed down in humble awe. After a silent pause, the impact of what they were seeing hit them. This was the promise of centuries; this was the fulfillment of ancient prophecies from Moses through Malachi!

The first shepherd was stricken with the incredible sight and the memory of the angelic announcement. Tears sprang to his eyes. He opened his mouth, fought momentarily to gain control of his voice, then whispered:

"Hosanna!"

The second shepherd echoed the word, slightly louder. "Hosanna!"

The third shepherd swept his arms wide in an all-encompassing motion of indescribable joy. "Hosanna! Hosanna!"

Outside, the bustling, torch-lit street of Bethlehem

seemed unaware of what had happened behind the crowded inn, in a cave stable. But the third shepherd burst through the entrance into the night and raised his hands in a glorious cry of adoration and delight. "Hosanna!" He ran through the crowds, shouting the word of praise to the Most High God. The other shepherds also sped into the night. They raced through the crowds and shouted so loudly that soon the crowd melted into knots of excited humanity.

"Hosanna! The Savior is born! The Messiah has come! Right here! In Bethlehem, as the prophet Malachi proclaimed centuries ago! The Savior is born—here in a manger!"

Some scoffed. They had fallen under the Hellenistic culture of the last three centuries, but Jews had never lost hope. The Messiah would come, they said. Others were annoyed. Some showed apathy. After all, they had been hearing about the Messiah's coming for centuries, and he had never come; why should they get excited over some shepherds' announcements? Would a king's birth be made known to such folk?

However, there were some who believed. They crowded close to the shepherds, listening, asking hushed, excited questions. Perhaps it was the joy written so plainly on the shepherds' faces. Perhaps it was the babbling retelling of the angelic announcement. But they believed.

These soon fanned out from the cave-stable and the inn, shouting in defiance of King Herod and the Roman occupation forces.

"Hosanna! Hosanna to God in the highest! The Savior is born!"

The little town of Bethlehem—and the world—would never again be the same.

CHAPTER FIVE

JERUSALEM'S STREETS were crowded with people doing business as usual. Roman soldiers stalked through the narrow, twisted, and dirty streets. Their nailed sandal-boots came down deliberately, methodically, in the careful, practiced manner of men ready to fight any instant.

Merchants shoved their way through the throngs, hurrying to set up their wares and turn a profit, while the sun climbed over the Mount of Olives. Priests made their way through the throngs, past the food stalls and small pack animals, which seemed to block every step.

Mary and Joseph seemed to flow through these obstructions without effort. Joseph carried Jesus toward the Temple. But first, Mary had to perform the ancient purification rites set down by Moses. She left Joseph and entered a private chamber.

Here she prepared herself for the first of a two-part

purification ritual. Mary slipped off her outer garment and approached the Temple Mikveh, in her long undergarment. A female bath attendant held out her arms. Mary passed the infant to the attendant. The new mother approached the Mikveh.

She entered the tublike container of water, which had been carved out of rock. Mary stood up to her shoulders near where the conduit led fresh water into the Mikveh.

Mary went through the cleansing ritual in obedience to God's words to Moses about a thousand years before. "If a woman conceives and bears a male child, then she shall not come into the sanctuary, until the days of her purifying are completed."

Mary rose from the waters, dried herself off, donned her outer garments and took the infant Jesus back. The second step of purification was easily completed: presentation and sacrifice of small birds.

The young mother rejoined Joseph. He took the baby and led the way through the Temple Court of the Gentiles. Now they would redeem the first-born son according to another ancient custom which had been laid out in the law.

The Temple Court of the Gentiles was noisy and bustling. Vendors hawked their wares. Jewish worshipers mingled with priests, Herodian soldiers, and Temple guards. Mary and Joseph caught a new meaning in the vendors' cries:

"Oxen! Oxen! Lambs! Best lambs for offering!"

Another tradesman called plaintively, "Only one left! One left!"

Mary and Joseph browsed along the rows of stalls. Joseph held Jesus close, away from the living, pulsating throng of humanity. The couples' eyes touched the rows of stalls: sellers of birds and sacrificial animals, plus money-changers' booths.

As they passed a pen of lambs, Joseph hesitated. His dark eyes caught Mary's. With a small sigh, the couple moved on.

At a money-changer's booth, Joseph pulled some Roman coins from his thin money pouch. The money-changer bowed his gratitude, as he exchanged the tainted money for temple shekels.

"The thirty-first day after birth, eh?"

Joseph nodded and Mary lowered her eyes.

The money-changer was in a good mood. "I gather you are not a kohen or a Levite, eh? And your wife is not the daughter of a kohen or Levite? Ah! Too bad! Then you would be exempt. But as it is—" the money-changer shrugged and turned to another customer with a cheerful greeting.

Mary and Joseph went on toward the Temple area where the kohen or priest would ask them the ritualistic questions, but there was still the offer of the sacrifice.

They passed a bird vendor. Mary's eyes lit up at the white birds in small, homemade cages of plaited switches.

"Joseph! This is good."

He mused aloud, "A pair of turtledoves, or two young pigeons."

It was the poor Jew's offering, specified in the time of Moses.

The vendor smiled at the baby, and asked his parents, "Then—you've come to dedicate the child?"

That, too, had been decreed in the distant past, yet the dedication of the first-born son was ever new and wonderful. Mary nodded to the vendor. He deftly placed the birds into a smaller cage of woven switches. With a sweep of his hands, the vendor offered the caged birds to Joseph. He handed the child to Mary and felt in his girdle for the untainted currency. The vendor bowed his gratitude and murmured, "May your son be a blessing."

Mary and Joseph turned away. As they moved toward the inner Temple court, the vendors' cries filled the air. "Pigeons! Turtledoves! Pigeons...."

At the Temple's inner court, the couple approached a white-robed priest. He stood at the gate to the inner court of the altar of sacrifice. It was an enormous rectangular altar about ten feet by twenty feet. There was a rim around the edge.

Mary handed Jesus to Joseph, since it was forbidden for women to enter the gate. She stepped back with a mother's reluctance. Joseph walked on alone and presented the child to the priest. Joseph cleared his throat nervously and made the ritual announcement.

"This is my first-born son, the first-born of his mother. The Holy One, blessed be He, has commanded to redeem him, as it is said: 'The redemption price for each first-born son of the age of one month shall be fixed at five sacred silver shekels at the rate of twenty gerahs.'"

Joseph hesitated, remembering, then continued quoting God's words about the dedication: "'Dedicate all the first-born males to me, for every first-born male Israelite and every first-born male animal belongs to me.'"

The priest asked his ritualistic questions with the tone of a man who had done it many times. "Do you prefer to give me your first-born son, the first-born of his mother, or would you rather redeem him for five shekels required by the Torah?"

Joseph said, "I prefer to redeem my son, and here is his redemption price required by the Torah."

The kohen received the untainted money and Joseph continued his part. "Blessed are Thou, Lord our God, King of the universe, who hast sanctified us with Thy commandments, and commanded us concerning the redemption of the first-born. Blessed art Thou, Lord our God, King of the universe, who hast granted us life and sustenance and permitted us to reach this season."

The priest held Jesus close to his chest with the left hand and raised the redemption money over the baby's head. "This instead of that, this in exchange for that, this is given up for that. May this child enjoy a life of Torah and godliness. Even as he has attained to redemption, so may he attain to the Torah, to the marriage canopy, and to a life of good deeds. Amen."

Joseph instinctively started to reach for Jesus, but the priest was not through. He placed his hand on the child's head and intoned: "May God make you like Ephraim and Manasseh. May the Lord bless you and take care of you; may the Lord be kind and gracious to you; may the Lord look on you with favor and give you peace."

The kohen was rushing now, completing the ritual with automatic words. "The Lord guards you; the Lord at your right hand is your shelter. A long and happy life will be given you. The Lord will guard you from all evil; he will guard your life. Amen."

Mary greeted Joseph as he returned, smiling broadly, and handed the dedicated Jesus to her. She took the infant with loving, motherly sounds. Joseph picked up the small bird cage. The couple started to walk away when an old, bearded gentleman in long, flowing robes stared at them. Satisfied, he tried to make his way toward them, but the milling crowd cut him off. He sighed and watched them again approach the Temple's inner court. Mary handed Jesus to Joseph, who walked off with Jesus in his arms and carrying the small bird cage in his right hand.

A white-robed priest opened the gate to the inner court. Joseph walked in and handed the birds to the priest. Joseph looked at the rectangular altar.

Joseph presented Jesus to the priest. Another white-robed priest took the sacrificial birds and handed them to a second similarly clad priest. The two men walked up a ramp and made the final, deft ritualistic motions. The newly dead birds were thrown into the flaming altar pyre.

Their tasks completed, Joseph and Mary with Jesus turned to leave. The old bearded Jew in flowing robes, who had tried to reach them before, was waiting. He accosted them and spoke to Mary.

"You are the mother of my Master."

It was more statement than question. Mary and Joseph looked at each other in wonder. Neither knew that this was Simeon, a righteous and devout Jerusalem resident who had long looked for what he called "the consolation of Israel." The Holy Spirit had revealed to Simeon that he would not see death before he had seen the Lord's Christ.

The old man reached out. Mary allowed him to take the child up in his arms. For a long moment, he gazed adoringly at the infant against his bony chest.

Simeon raised his watery old eyes in worship. His gray beard quivered with intense emotion. "Now, Lord, you have kept your promise, and you may let your servant go in peace!"

Mary and Joseph exchanged wondering looks.

"With my own eyes," Simeon softly continued, "I have seen your salvation, which you have prepared in the presence of all peoples...."

Simeon's voice trembled and threatened to break, but it grew stronger as he continued. "A light to reveal your will to the Gentiles and bring glory to your people Israel."

The watery old eyes, bright with grateful tears, fastened gently upon Mary's young countenance. Simeon's voice changed. It was firm, convincing.

"This child is chosen by God for the destruction and the salvation of many in Israel. He will be a sign from God which many people will speak against, and so reveal their secret thoughts. And sorrow, like a sharp sword, will break your own heart."

A look of concern shadowed Mary's face. She

reached instinctively for the infant. Simeon handed
Jesus back to her. His eyes streamed with tears. His
words followed, "May you both be blessed." He turned
away.

An old woman entirely dressed in black had been
watching. She had begun to move forward, as Simeon
surrendered the baby to Mary. As the old man shuffled
slowly away, the old woman fastened her eyes on the
child as if making sure of positive identification.

"He's the one!" Her trembling voice startled Mary
and Joseph. "The redemption—the Savior!" the old
woman added with emphasis.

Her crooked forefinger, thin with great age, pointed
at Jesus. Then her eyes swept up in a movement of great
resolution. "I must tell everyone," she said, turning to
the crowd. "I must tell everyone I have seen him."

Joseph and Mary stood bewildered. A matronly
woman with deep furrows in her full face leaned close
and whispered reassuringly to the couple. "Don't mind
her! That's just Anna the prophetess. She's eighty-four,
you know, and a widow for most of her life. She never
leaves the Temple." The matron frowned, gazing
thoughtfully after the widow. "I wonder what she
meant about telling everyone she has seen... *him?*"

Chapter Six

By THE TIME he was twelve, Jesus had developed into a sturdy, muscular boy. He worked in his father's carpenter's shop at Nazareth. He was familiar with the tools which hung on the wall: plummet, awl, adze, set square, and chisels. He was using a bow drill with easy familiarity, making a cart transom at his father's workbench.

Jesus picked up the transom and walked past newly made or repaired wooden plows, stools, and other simple items. Outside the shop, Jesus nailed the transom to the back of an absolutely decrepit cart.

At the other end of the cart, a man, in no better condition than his vehicle, stood absently stroking his donkey's muzzle.

At the front of their small house, Joseph was securing bundles to his own donkey's back. He looked up, as travelers moved purposefully by. Men and women's voices came to the carpenter.

"I've forgotten the water jars! Do we go back for them, or trust we'll find sufficient water on the way to Jerusalem?"

A young woman called to her small child, "Don't get lost! Stay with your mother, until we reach Jerusalem."

Mary came out of the house carrying a small linen parcel. She closed the door behind her and approached her husband. He looked up with a pleased smile.

"We're almost ready to go. Jesus is mending the teacher's cart. When he's gone, Jesus can handle the other jobs on hand."

Mary handed the parcel to her husband. He looked inquisitively at it, then pulled back a flap to reveal the loaf of specially prepared bread called *matzoh*. It was a very flat bread, eight to ten inches across, round in shape, so hard it cracked when broken, and tasted so uninteresting it would not willingly have been eaten for flavor—because it didn't have any.

Mary explained, "The Passover bread."

Joseph covered the parcel and carefully tucked it into the donkey's bundles. Joseph's fingers lingered on the linen parcel. He said over his shoulder, "Jesus is almost of age. Perhaps this year he should travel with the men . . . ?"

Joseph turned around, seeking information for a decision he obviously had already made:

Mary smiled approval. Joseph grinned and started for the carpenter shop calling, "Jesus?"

Jerusalem was much more crowded at Passover than Mary and Joseph had experienced a dozen years before at Bethlehem, when the inns were full and only the cave manger had provided shelter. Every Jewish man, who could, had traveled to the capital city for the spring feast and celebration.

Tents had sprung up all over the surrounding hills above the ancient city. The pilgrims were so thick that the Roman legions, traditionally moved to Jerusalem to assure order, had to pick their way carefully around the makeshift shelters which sprawled even around the Temple itself.

Many things had happened in the last few years. Herod the king had died a few years ago of a terrible disease. The third of his sons had been executed at the old man's orders, just five days before Herod died. Archelaus, a surviving son, had been barely eighteen when he succeeded the old tyrant. Archelaus never became king; Caesar Augustus had given him the lesser title of ethnarch. His full-brother, Antipas, who became the tetrarch Herod, had contested their father's will. In the end, Archelaus had ruled only six years in Judea. He had recently been deposed by the emperor. Roman procurators now governed in Judea. Herod Antipas continued to reign as tetrarch in Galilee. A half-brother, Philip, one of the many children born to the late king Herod and his ten wives, ruled quietly in the far northern provinces of Perea and Trachonitis.

Two years after the old king's death, Judah the Galanite (son of the bandit, Hezekiah, whom Herod had executed in the early days of his reign) had led a revolt. With Zadok the Pharisee, Judah had formed a group who were zealous for the Lord. It wasn't a party as such, but was organized to protest a census taken by Cyrenius, governor of Syria. The patriotic Zealots claimed they owed allegiance only to God. These Zealots had been hardly more than a series of buzzing flies to the imperial troops of Rome. The movement was crushed, as mentioned previously.

Hillel, the great Jewish rabbi, still sat as head of the Great Council (the *Sanhedrin* in Greek), and was the Jewish religious authority of seventy or so men. Hillel would remain at the head of the Council until he died, and that probably would be soon. He was an old man now, revered and honored for his wisdom and pithy sayings.

Every Jew knew the political-religious situation was most sensitive at the Passover, when all the world seemed to converge on Jerusalem to celebrate the liberation of the Hebrews under Moses. Centuries before, he had performed miracles before Pharaoh. But only when the first-born of every Egyptian home had died in the same night had Pharaoh let the Hebrews go. Death had passed over the Hebrews, however, and not one Hebrew had died. Moses led his people from Egyptian slavery to become a new nation at Sinai. The Hebrews had been a nation before they had one square foot of the Promised Land. And they had never forgotten the Passover.

The descendants of Sinai's wilderness wanderings had conquered the land promised by God to Abraham long before Moses' time. Since then, ten of the twelve tribes had vanished into the Assyrian deportation. More than a century later the last surviving tribe, Judah, had been deported to Babylonia. Not all of the people had been deported, but those exiled had been important. They included mostly the intellectuals and the professionals, the leadership, and the rich.

How many were actually deported in each case? Sargon, in the Assyrian annals, claims he exiled only 27,290 persons. There were more than 60,000 landowners in Israel at the time of deportation. Some Israelites were never carried off to Assyria at all. Nebuchadnezzar took from Jerusalem the princes, the mighty men of valor (10,000 captives), the craftsmen and smiths, so that those who remained were the poorest sort of people in the land. The deportees were collectively Hebrews.

The Persians, who succeeded the Babylonians, were lenient to the exiles among them and allowed a measure of self-government. Most were content to stay in exile, but some wanted to return. After all, the Promised Land was theirs by God's own promise. So some exiles received permission to return to Jerusalem as Jews. All those years, from then to now, the messianic hope had grown. On Passover, when Jesus was twelve years old, the Jews were still hopeful; still looking for the changes that would come when the Messiah came. And the messianic expectation was higher than ever.

Mary, standing by an open window overlooking the quiet city, brushed these thoughts from her mind. No one was in the streets except the legionnaires. Everyone was inside this night, enacting a ritual that would continue for some through the centuries.

Mary's eyes focused on the scene inside the room.

Joseph, Jesus, a teacher, and seven others sat on pillows on the floor, resting on their left hands. They reclined at the table in the Greek and Roman custom of free men. A small child also reclined before the low table. They would eat only with their right hands, whether they were right or left-handed. The table was set with the best pottery and oil lamps. In the middle of the platters of food, the matzoh rested on a piece of linen.

The teacher began the ancient ritual. "Blessed art Thou, O Lord our God, King of the Universe, who bringeth forth fruit of the vine from the earth."

There were softly murmured *amens* all around.

Joseph raised a piece of matzoh. "Behold, this is the bread of affliction which our forefathers ate in the land of Egypt." Joseph paused, then continued the blessing over bread. "Blessed art Thou, Lord our God, King of the Universe, who bringeth forth bread from the earth." Again, Joseph paused briefly and then added, "Blessed art Thou, Lord our God, King of the Universe, who hath sanctified us with His commandments, and commanded concerning the eating of matzoh."

He looked around at the guests, then added: "Let all who are hungry come in and eat. Let all who want to, observe the Passover. This year as slaves; next year as free men!"

Mary watched with deeply felt emotion as the small child turned to the teacher with the first of the "Four Questions."

"Why is this night different from other nights?"

The child's dark eyes reflected the cheerful flames

from the oil lamps. He raised his voice slightly as he overcame his self-consciousness.

"For on other nights we eat seasoned food once, but this night twice; on other nights we eat leavened or unleavened bread, but this night all is unleavened; on other nights we eat flesh roast, stewed or cooked, but this night all is roast."

It was a ritual quotation. The truth was that most people were so poor they rarely ate meat. But the four questions were standard, covering the thoughts "Why this night ... why do we eat seasoned food ... why unleavened bread ... why roasted meat?"

The ritualistic answer came from the teacher's lips. "We were once slaves of Pharaoh in Egypt, but the Lord our God brought us out from there with a mighty hand and an outstretched arm.

"Had not God brought our fathers out of Egypt, our children and grandchildren would still be slaves."

After the meal, the assembled company concluded with the Seder prayer: "Therefore, O Lord our God and the God of our fathers, bring us in peace to the other set feasts and festivals which are coming to meet us, while we rejoice in the building up of Thy city and and are joyful in Thy worship; and may we eat there of the sacrifices and of the Passover-offerings whose blood has reached with acceptance the wall of Thy altar, and let us praise Thee for our redemption and for the ransoming of our souls. Blessed are Thou, O Lord, who hast redeemed Israel!"

The low table was littered with remnants of the

meal. Jesus, as any boy who's had an exciting day, struggled to keep awake. He nestled against Joseph's shoulder.

The great throngs stayed in Jerusalem until the full eight days had been observed. Then the Jews began streaming out of Jerusalem, heading in all directions to their homes. There was so much bustle in the massive caravan which Mary and Joseph joined in their trek toward Nazareth, that they thought Jesus was with friends. They had gone about a day's journey, when Mary and Joseph realized Jesus was not in the caravan. They quickly made a final search of friends and relatives. Confirming with dismay that nobody had seen the twelve-year-old boy, Mary and Joseph frantically hurried back toward Jerusalem to search for him.

On the third day, the boy Jesus sat on stone steps in one corner of the great Temple court. The priests and other religious leaders surrounding him were astonished at Jesus' precociousness.

Joseph and Mary hurried into the courtyard entrance. They were frightened, after three days of fruitless searching.

"There!" Joseph grabbed his wife's arm and pointed. The parents ran toward Jesus. He was saying to a rabbi, "... Since the Messiah is a three-fold manifestation, perhaps the prophet, the priest, and the king will be embodied in one man. Could that be?"

The rabbi stroked his beard. "Why does one so young ask?"

Before Jesus could answer, a second looked around. "Whose child is this," he demanded, "who asks such questions?"

Joseph stepped forward. "He's from Nazareth. We thought he had left with us. Please forgive his zeal."

The second rabbi frowned in annoyance, but the first teacher smiled broadly and said, "Look after him! He has understanding and the rare beginnings of wisdom. Peace be with you."

Joseph managed a faint smile. For days, he had been fearful for Jesus' safety and whereabouts. Now a surge of combined relief and annoyance swept over him. But before he could speak, Mary leaned down to Jesus and asked, "Son, why have you done this to us? Your father and I have been terribly worried trying to find you."

Jesus looked up at his mother and answered, "Why did you have to look for me? Didn't you know that I had to be in my Father's house?"

Mary and Joseph exchanged puzzled glances. They shook their heads, briefly. They didn't understand what Jesus meant.

"Come, Son," Joseph said, placing a hand on Jesus' young shoulders. "Let's go back to Nazareth."

CHAPTER SEVEN

EIGHTEEN YEARS later, John, the son of Zechariah and Elizabeth, startled the whole Jewish population. He came out of the Judean wilderness and began preaching and baptizing in the River Jordan. His activities soon were discussed from the lowest water bearer and hewer of wood to the procurators in Jerusalem and the tetrarch in Galilee.

John took an ancient Jewish ceremonial washing specified in the Torah (and one used by Jews to initiate proselytes into Israel) and gave it such unique emphasis, that soon he was called John the Baptist.

John preached with such fervor and conviction that soon Pharisees and Sadducees and the old and young of the land flocked to the rivers where John was baptizing. For more than a man held sway; the possibility of John's being either the Messiah or his forerunner was hotly discussed.

John the Baptist was different in his dress, manner, and food. He reminded the people of their old-time prophets, who had spoken out boldly in past centuries, speaking God's words of warning to a people who had sometimes drifted from their earlier teachings. The way John the Baptist behaved reminded the people of Elijah.

Elijah, the Tishbite, the dynamic ninth-century prophet from the northern kingdom, had been unconventional in dress. He was described as hairy, with a leather girdle. Elijah was also of rugged physical constitution and had a habit of dwelling in caves.

This prophet had shaped history and still dominated Jewish thinking. He had not died, but been carried into heaven by a whirlwind. It was commonly expected he would come again to help Israel prepare for the coming of the Messiah.

But was John the Baptist the Messiah or the Elijah-like forerunner? The Jews watching John in the Jordan argued heatedly about the subject. The believers were tempted to heed John's call, but the skeptics sat on the bank and sneered in disbelief. The wild-looking man stripped off his camel's hair garment and wide girdle and tucked up his underclothes in what was called "girding his loin," then waded into the river. John called out, "Turn away from your sins and be baptized, and God will forgive your sins!"

John's voice was powerful and commanding, totally unlike his thin, ascetic body. Looking at him, it was easy to believe that he had lived a long time in the desert, eating locusts and wild honey. His black hair was uncut and full in the Nazarite way. It spilled down around his thin, bony cheeks and blended with the fierce, black beard. There was a tendency to call him a wild man, yet there was such power and conviction in his voice, that he moved whole multitudes to action.

"Repent!" John shouted. "Be baptized!" The young, the old, the sighted and blind, the lame and the healthy began to peel off their outer garments. They waded into the river in droves. As John's authoritative tones rang out over the waters, the people baptized themselves in the river and waded across to the opposite bank. It was a simple act, but it bore great symbolism to those who had obeyed John.

He turned to face those still on the banks. "Turn away from your sins and be baptized, and God will forgive your sins! As it is written in the book of the prophet Isaiah: 'Someone is shouting in the desert: Get the road ready for the Lord.'"

That was a stirring declaration. The listeners shuffled uneasily, for John was making a direct association with ancient prophecies involving the Messiah's coming.

Roman and Herodian soldiers sensed the Jews' rising interest. The soldiers watched, as John waded from the shallows and stood, dripping and alone, on a rock ledge overhanging the river. The people were reminded of the words of the prophet Isaiah:

"...make a straight path for him to travel! Every valley must be filled up, every hill and mountain leveled off. The winding roads must be made straight, and the rough paths made smooth. All mankind will see God's salvation!"

John picked up his knee-length camel's hair tunic

and wide girdle, as though to dress and depart when the tiny rivulets of water quit dripping off his body and splattering on the rock. He picked up his stout staff from where he had laid it and regarded the multitudes, who stood indecisively or in plain curiosity upon the banks.

"You snakes!"

The sharp word quieted the throngs.

"Who told you that you could escape from the punishment God is about to send?"

Some people naturally resented John's remark. Others looked at one another in growing embarrassment. The ascetic's deep-brown eyes seemed to settle on each man individually, sweeping aside the cloak of respectability each had wrapped about himself, and to see the innermost darkness of each one's heart.

Some spectators felt a tingle of fear, as the baptizer's probing eyes bore deeply into them. Wordlessly, the more convinced removed their sandals and began tucking their tunics up for baptism. This knee-length undergarment, worn next to the skin, was usually of wool. It had sleeves, plus a leather girdle at the waist. Since it was summer, no one wore cloak or mantle, in which the poor often slept, and which provided the outer garment for rainy or cold weather.

The baptizer seemed more concerned with those who hesitated. Some of these were Pharisees or Sadducees, two of the three principal Jewish religious sects.

The Pharisees were craftsmen who wore their trade emblems as a badge of their occupation. The scribe carried his reed pen behind an ear. The tailor's strand of wool attached to his tunic advertised his skill. There was a great deal of misunderstanding about the Pharisees. There were some great and noble ones. They took their religion seriously. The Pharisees had a genuine devotion to a way of life designed to elevate the Jewish community from the plane of history to the realm of eternity.

The Pharisees believed God loved the individual so much, that He revealed His will so that the individual might hope for eternal life and resurrection. This was not a political notion. It was an explanation of what life was all about. In the Greco-Roman world, life was something that needed explaining. The Pharisees wanted a way to bring the Kingdom of God down to earth. For them, that was the Law.

The Pharisees believed that one's place in the Kingdom of God counted for something, and one could take one's place in the Kingdom by observing the Law.

The rabbis stressed two religio-legal issues: Sabbath observance and ritual purity.

As their name implied, Pharisees were "separated." Their central belief was in a certain set of purity requirements. They held to the oral law, in addition to the written one. They believed in the resurrection of the dead. They favored a Messiah from the house of David. There were only six thousand Pharisees altogether, according to Josephus, the historian.

There were even fewer Sadducees who were associated with the priesthood. Some were wealthy, but not all. They considered the written Law, the Prophets, and Writings as holy. But they rejected the oral law as invalid, and they did not believe in an afterlife or angels. Their outlook on life was religious. Basically, the Sadducees could be said to be defenders of priestly prerogatives.

The Jews generally believed that the priests were the only legitimate representatives of God's Kingdom on earth. The right of the priests to rule was firmly grounded in the Old Testament. The Temple, as the central or critical component of Judaism, was in the priests' hands. And, in the opinion of the people, that's where it belonged.

The Sadducees believed in the Messiah, possibly like Moses, as prophet; or one of priestly descent, like Zadok. The Sadducees third alternative was a Messiah from the house of David.

Neither of the two principal religious groups were too likely to cooperate with the Romans. This was a violation of the heredity right of the priests to rule. The Romans were prone to desecrate the Temple, which was a religious horror to the Jews in general and the priests in particular.

The Essenes, the third Jewish religious sect, tended to a separatist life. They lived apart in a community called *Qumran*, near the Dead Sea, and rarely mingled with the other Jewish groups. Some people thought John was really an Essene, for he was certainly more like them than like the Sadducees or Pharisees.

John clenched his long, thin fingers about the staff and continued his exhortation.

"Do those things that will show that you have turned from your sins!"

The persuasive power of John's voice caused some Roman soldiers to shift uneasily. They gripped their shields and weapons from their vantage points above him on the shore. Ever since the Zealots had sprung up a couple years after Herod the king had died, a rising fever of rebellion had swept through both Judea and Galilee.

Several Roman procurators had come and gone in Judea. None had stopped the stirring sense of patriotism which permeated the land. Not even Pontius Pilate, the current Judean governor, had been able to stop the Jews' stubborn but quiet resistance to the Roman occupation forces.

It wasn't that Pilate hadn't tried. He had once offended the Jews by bringing the Roman standards into Jerusalem at night. When the Jews saw the standards, they raised a great outcry over the idolatrous symbols to which legionnaires bowed in worship. Even the threat of glistening, naked Roman swords had not caused the Jews to back down from their demands that the hated symbols of idolatry be removed. Thousands of Jews had offered their naked throats to the swords. Pilate had backed down. The standards had been removed.

John's tremendous voice rose again, so everyone standing on the Jordan's banks looked at him with a mixture of conviction, skepticism, or concern.

"The ax is ready to cut down the trees at the roots: every tree that does not bear good fruit will be cut down and thrown into the fire."

Again, the crowds stirred uneasily. Many shuffled forward in dusty sandals to indicate their willingness to believe his message.

Others hesitated, skeptical and cautious, but still wondering about the source of authority for this one lone, scrawny young man. He had come out of nowhere and was now shaking the whole of Judea and Galilee with his blunt accusations against wrongdoing and his invitation to repent and be baptized.

No place was safe from the penetrating voice of John the Baptist. His message of condemnation had even seeped through the great fortress-prison at Machaerus. This mighty bastion of rich and powerful rulers had been built by Alexander Jannasus, the Maccabean whose family had routed the Greeks under Antiochus IV (Epiphanes).

At Machaerus, Herod Antipas stirred uneasily. His father had strengthened Machaerus where it overlooked the north-south road to Damascus and overlooking the northeast Dead Sea shores in Peraea. It was safe from military assault, but not the voice of John the Baptist.

What John the Baptist proclaimed on both sides of the Jordan struck tender spots inside the tetrarch's fortress.

Herod the tetrarch, sat in his administrative office with his wife, Herodias, and an aide, Chuza. A Roman battle scene behind them served as a decoration on a cold, stone wall. He wore the *toga praetexta*, a Roman toga of wool, lavishly draped over the left shoulder, and falling richly to the ankles.

Ordinarily, Herod Antipas would only have worn the imperial toga for ceremonial use. But there were disturbing rumors in the air, and he wore the garment now for the symbolism it carried: the outward emblem of an invincible and ruthless conqueror in Rome, whom he represented in Galilee.

Herod Antipas was graying, with loose curls lightly falling over his furrowed brow. He was balding in back. His beard was short, a concession to the Jewish subjects who were generally bearded, and yet close enough to the Roman custom of being clean-shaven.

Herod reached a fleshy hand with a huge gold ring and deposited a rolled parchment on a table already strewn with many others.

"Calm yourself," he said, turning to his wife. "You're quite overwrought."

Herodias, in her late thirties, still showed evidence that she had been a beautiful woman. When she had been married to Philip, a half-brother to Antipas, her striking beauty had caused Antipas to propose marriage. She had divorced her ambitious husband, new tetrarch in the north, and taken her teenage daughter, Salome, to marry the ruler of Galilee. This had incensed the Jews, because their laws forbade a man marrying his brother's wife while he lived. Such a marriage was also illegal, if the woman had borne a child of the first brother.

Now, even in her anger, Herodias still showed some of the loveliness which had caused Antipas to risk the Jews' anger. She had long, dark eyelashes and a full, nondelicate nose. Her sensuous lips were richly red with color. Her shoulders were bare and smooth where the toga *pura* fell from ornate gold clasps.

Herodias's still-black hair was piled high on her head in an elaborate styling. Row upon row of exquisite curls soared away from the curling dark bangs over her forehead. Gold and turquoise jewelry sparkled from her hair, her throat, and arms. She wore several expensive rings on her fingers. Herodias stormed, "He has defamed our marriage on more than one occasion!"

Herod framed a question with a slight edge, intended to rouse further animosity in Herodias. "Slandered my brother's wife?"

Herodias snapped, "I am *your* wife, Herod!"

The tetrarch slowly drew in a breath through his large nostrils. He knew where the conversation was again headed. He moved to change the direction.

"I can't have him killed, Herodias. He's a holy man."

Herodias snorted in a most unladylike way. "A vexatious Jew! Before long they'll embrace him as their...." She paused, searching for the Roman word, but finally settled on the Hebrew: "Messiah."

"The Christ? Perish the thought!"

Herodias opened her bright red lips in anger, but controlled her words. She gazed thoughtfully at her husband from under long, dark eyelashes. She had been married to the tetrarch long enough to know his words and convictions didn't always meld. He had heard enough about the captivating power John the Baptist had over the masses. Herod's blue-clad soldiers had relayed to him the rumors that John might be the promised Messiah, who would somehow rule where Herod now ruled. This Messiah—if he had come or was coming—was a threat to Herod. But he was afraid to take open action against John for fear of the Jews.

"My husband!" Herodias lowered her voice to a sultry, insinuating level and tried a more devious approach to gain her goal: John's death. Herodias cupped his hand in hers. One large turquoise ring on her finger touched his fingers. Her wide, gold and gem-encrusted bracelet dangled against his flesh, as she placed a long, lingering kiss on his lips.

Herod stirred in response. He reached for her in rising hunger, but she slipped deftly from his grasp.

"Arrest him for me!" she cried.

Herod sighed. He should have known! Herodias had all the wiles of a beautiful, sought-after woman; she also knew how to get what she wanted.

Herod called, "Chuza!"

The officer of his guard straightened; he had been unobtrusively preparing to drip wax on a fresh parchment for Herod's seal.

Chuza wore the *paludamentum*, a red cloak which distinguished him from wartime citizens who wore the smaller *sagum*. His was fringed with purple and made a startling contrast to his armor. He drew himself up in the stiff, formal attitude of a soldier about to receive an unwelcome order.

Herodias reached past her elaborate gold-and-emerald necklace, to gently touch the piles of black curls which rose magnificently from her scheming head. She smiled to herself and left her husband instructing Chuza.

It had clouded over, and the Jordan was in shadows. But John was again standing chest-deep in the waters of the Jordan and calling the Jews to baptism. A squad of Roman soldiers squirmed in the shade and wished for sundown, so they could return to barracks. But they kept their hard eyes on the thin, emaciated man in the water.

John called to the throngs on the shore in his powerful, compelling voice.

"Turn away from your sins and be baptized!"

John's familiar call seemed to have a magical effect on the ordinary people. They responded to his invitation. They also waded into the stream, immersed themselves and rose, streaming water and smiling with some inner secret or knowledge. They climbed out on the opposite shore.

John waded out of the Jordan to the shore and addressed those still standing uncertainly.

"God will forgive your sins," he said with quiet power.

There was now no thunder, no volume of voice, yet the power was still there. The dark eyes and the strength of his conviction moved a Jew in the crowd to respond.

He asked, "What should we do?"

John seemed not to hear, as his dark, commanding eyes noticed a poor man in rags. Then the baptizer turned the full force of his magnetic eyes on the man who had asked the question. John's voice rumbled deep from within the thin, hairy chest.

"Whoever has two shirts must give one to the man who has none, and whoever has food must share it."

Far back in the crowd, someone spoke with sudden,

positive conviction. "He's the Messiah."

The word was like a coal from a brazier touched to dry papyrus. It became an echo sweeping through the crowd.

"The Messiah! He's the Messiah!"

The word gathered strength, fanned by the hot breath of strong belief. "The Messiah! The Messiah has come at last!"

Before the flames of conviction could sweep the length of the crowd and reach John's ears, two corpulent men with girded loins approached the baptizer.

"Teacher," one said respectfully.

John's black eyes fastened on the men.

The first one whispered, "We're tax collectors. What should we do?"

John smiled at the Jews, who were hated by their countrymen, because they gathered taxes for the hated Romans and always collected more than the required amount as their profit.

John replied, "Don't collect more than is legal!"

A couple of blue-clad Herodian soldiers, moved by the strange power in John's voice, stepped forward. The taller one asked, "What about us? What are we to do?"

"Don't take money from anyone by force, or accuse anyone falsely." The baptizer paused and added, "Be content with your pay."

As the soldiers reacted with a mixture of half-smiles and deep concern, a solitary figure approached the river on the opposite bank. He was about thirty years old, with long, dark hair spilling down both sides of his strong, sensitive face. Although all the Jews were Hellenized to some extent, with some shaving their faces and cutting their hair short in the Greco-Roman fashion, this man wore a full beard, in the traditional Jewish manner. He began removing his simple one-piece white robe to gird his loins. John caught the newcomer's actions out of the corner of his eye.

John began moving toward the water to supervise this man's baptism.

But John's eyes were on the crowd, where someone finally asked him the question that had seared through their ranks with growing intensity.

"Are you the Christ?"

The crowd echoed their bolder member's question. John stopped them with an upraised hand.

"I baptize you with water, but someone is coming who is much greater than I am."

The crowd stirred uncertainly. Did that mean he was or was not the Anointed One?

John made his position plain.

"I am not good enough even to untie his sandals. He will baptize you with the Holy Spirit and fire."

Behind John, the figure with girded loins stepped into the waters and began wading across the Jordan toward John, who was continuing his explanation to the crowd.

"He has his winnowing shovel with him, to thresh out all the grain and gather the wheat into his barn; but he will burn the chaff in a fire that never goes out."

John turned at the sound of the approaching baptismal candidate.

John recognized Jesus.

He drew abreast of John. John instantly stepped back a pace in awe. But Jesus quietly stood before him, awaiting baptism. John started to protest, but Jesus bowed his head. John baptized him.

Suddenly, a shaft of golden light burst through the clouds. The light seemed to settle on Jesus in a unique way, so that the crowd murmured in surprise.

A pure white dove descended on spotless wings and fluttered to rest on Jesus' left shoulder.

Suddenly, some of those standing near glanced apprehensively at the sky. They thought they heard thunder. Others heard a voice; a deep, rich tone of incredible strength, blended with gentleness and pride.

"You are my own dear Son. I am pleased with you."

Those farthest from the baptizer and Jesus looked uncertainly at the sky. Had it thundered? Or had they heard the voice of the invisible God who had spoken from Sinai centuries before?

That night, John and some of his disciples were camped by the river when Chuza rode horseback into the campfire's circle of light.

A cadre of Herodian foot soldiers appeared with torches from behind a rocky blind. Chuza wordlessly indicated John, by pointing with Herod's arrest parchment.

Instantly, John's disciples scattered in fear. But John

slowly stood to face the troops.

Two soldiers seized the baptizer's arms. He did not resist. He walked uprightly into the night, surrounded by Chuza's foot soldiers.

Chapter Eight

THE JUDEAN wilderness was blasted by the summer sun. The parched, rugged, and forbidding terrain seemed to be entirely without life. But in all that vast emptiness, among the blistering heat and the great empty silence, one lone man moved. Jesus was so tiny a figure compared to the tremendous solitude and emptiness of the desert that he seemed to be as a grain of sand among countless miles of tumbled boulders.

His face was cracked and gaunt. After forty days and nights alone, his simple off-white-colored robe was dust covered. His eyes, dark and recessed in the caverns of his weary face, seemed to be the only part of him still alive. His body was sucked by the incessant heat of the wilderness. But still he lived—alone, in all that terrible solitude—he lived; yet not without a terrible penalty for the solitude of preparation. And his ordeal was not over.

With effort, he ran his thick, dry tongue across his cracked, painful lips. His tongue stuck; it was no less dry than the lips.

Perhaps if he put a pebble in his mouth and sucked on it? Tentatively, Jesus reached out for a small, weathered stone. The shadow of his thin fingers raced ahead of his slowly moving hand to grasp the pebble.

A voice stopped the hand abruptly; the shadow froze above the pebble.

"If you *are* God's Son, order this stone to turn into bread."

Jesus withdrew his hand and looked around. Only the oppressive emptiness of the desert wilderness met his eyes. Yet there was something ominous in the dry air; a voice with the beguiling, smoothly convincing tones of Satan, making something seem logical when it was not. Jesus forced his cracked lips to move; the clacking tongue in his dry mouth moved.

"The scripture says, 'Man cannot live on bread alone.'"

Jesus got slowly, wearily, to his feet. He walked purposefully away.

Some time later, his head was bent with effort. Every step was in agony. Then something caught his bloodshot eyes. Jesus raised his head with great difficulty.

He looked across the empty void of the desert, where a mirage seemed to be forming. As Jesus stared, a colossal, translucent city began to materialize. It rolled back across the desert, shimmering, beautiful in the merciless sunlight. Jesus paused, one tired foot in front of the other, appreciating the spectacle.

The voice came again: soft, smooth and very convincing. "I will give you all this power and all this wealth. It has all been handed over to me, and I can give it to anyone I choose."

The silky voice paused, then added: "All this will be yours, then, if you worship me."

The voice was so logical, so believable, so totally convincing. No ordinary rebuff would suffice to still it. Jesus forced his thick tongue to move in the dry cavern of his mouth. He willed his painfully cracked lips to form a suitable reply.

"The scripture says, 'Worship the Lord your God and serve only him!'"

The voice was silent again; as silent as the great desert itself. But that night, when resistance was at its lowest ebb, the smooth, convincing voice came again.

Jesus found himself standing on the very edge of the highest point of the Jerusalem Temple. Jesus' frayed, gritty sandals seemed to be touching the very edge of the precipice. It seemed as though at any moment he would hurl himself down. The torchlights below reflected the agony of his tortured features.

The voice was so believable! "If you are God's Son, throw yourself down from here!"

Jesus hesitated, looking at the Temple courtyard far below.

The satanic voice continued, beguiling and rational. "If you are God's Son, throw yourself down from here! For the scripture says, 'God will order his angels to take good care of you.' It also says, 'They will hold you up with their hands so that not even your feet will be hurt on the stones.'"

Jesus stepped back and reached into his memory for the strongest defensive weapon available. "The scripture says," Jesus replied, "'Do not put the Lord your God to the test!'"

Jesus drew his tired body upright. The clear, fresh breath of life blew by his numbed, fatigued brain and refreshed him. "The scripture says..." he started to repeat, but it wasn't necessary.

He was alone.

The weariness had vanished. Slowly, carefully, but with increasing evidence of surging new strength, Jesus climbed down to safety.

The temptations were past—for now.

Jesus was ready for his life work.

The Jewish synagogue at Nazareth in Galilee of the Gentiles was about to start sermons. Two latecomers, in full beards and in the simple garments of the people, quickly found places. Around them were scholars, merchants, and laborers. They respectfully sat on the floor or on the stone steps along the walls.

The women were in the rear of the synagogue, behind a wooden lattice screen. This was designed to prevent a man from accidentally touching a menstruant and becoming unclean.

The synagogue leader scanned the front row of men sitting on the hard-packed earth floor. His eyes settled on Jesus.

"Will you read the Law?"

Jesus rose thoughtfully and mounted the three steps to the platform.

He received the scroll from the attendant and opened it to the place he wanted. Jesus, now without any trace of the dry, parched lips he had recently experienced in his wilderness temptation, began to read in clear, strong baritone.

"The Spirit of the Lord is upon me, because he has chosen me to bring good news to the poor."

The listeners nodded with appreciation of the familiar words from the prophet Isaiah. How often they had heard these words, written centuries before! But, as always, there was something meaningful in the passage. Today, there was something different about the words. Perhaps it was the way Jesus' face shone with an inner conviction which was projected with his reading.

"He has sent me to proclaim liberty to the captives," Jesus continued, barely glancing at the memorized characters on the scroll, "and recovery of sight to the blind, to set free the oppressed and . . ." Jesus hesitated, looking over the congregation before adding, ". . . announce that the time has come when the Lord will save his people."

Behind the rear screen, a woman peered through the latticework at Jesus and whispered to a friend, "Isn't that Joseph's son?"

Standing at the reading desk, with the three doors of the synagogue closed behind him, Jesus rolled up the scroll and kissed it. He handed it back to the attendant.

"This passage of scripture," Jesus announced with

clear, authoritative tones, "has come true today, as you heard it being read."

A man on a stone bench to the right leaned to his right and whispered to a friend, "Did he say the Scripture had come true?"

His friend pursed his whiskered lips in disapproval. "Only the Messiah can fulfill. . . ." He didn't finish, for Jesus was speaking again.

"I am sure that you will quote this proverb to me, 'Doctor, heal yourself.' You will also tell me to do here in my home town the same things you heard were done in. . . ." Jesus paused, seeming to think of an example. "Capernaum," he added.

The congregation stirred with surprise. Jesus seemed not to notice. His voice reached powerfully across the men in front, past the screen in back to the woman in the farthest corner. "I tell you this; a prophet is never welcomed in his home town. . . ."

An old graybeard interrupted, "What kind of blasphemy is this?"

A younger man rose to his feet. "What's he saying?"

The other worshipers rose together with cries of "Blasphemy!"

Their outraged reaction turned from words to action. They moved resolutely toward Jesus.

A moment later, the crowd spilled out of the synagogue doorway, pushing Jesus roughly ahead of them. Angrily, with loud cries and furious motions, they surrounded, pushed, and jostled Jesus through the street.

A small, wide-eyed child glanced up from his

playing, as the crowd's fury surged by him, along the narrow, crooked, and dirty streets.

The mob, stirred to fury because of the conviction Jesus had committed the sin of blasphemy, hurried him toward the edge of town. Blasphemy was a capital offense, for which death by stoning was specified. The custom was to shove the victim over the cliff and drop rocks on him, or throw rocks down, until he was dead.

But somehow, Jesus mysteriously slipped through the angry, shoving mob. When they reached the cliff's edge, Jesus was gone. The people swirled in surprised and angry little eddies of righteous indignation within the larger current of religious zealots. But it was useless; they couldn't find Jesus.

By the time the groups' anger cooled and they began drifting in mystified small knots back toward town, Jesus had come to a fork in the trail well out of sight from the Nazarene villagers. One path led back down the hill toward Nazareth. The other led away, into the fertile, green Galilean hills.

Without hesitancy, Jesus turned away from Nazareth. He walked steadily, until he was a tiny movement against the distant horizon.

Without even a walking stick, Jesus left his hometown to begin fulfilling the words he had read in the synagogue.

CHAPTER NINE

NEAR SUNSET, Jesus proceeded along a dusty road. He saw an old woman in front of a small house. She lay on a bed set under a ragged awning. She tossed restlessly, stirred by a fever, which soaked her worn face with perspiration. Jesus moved up to her couch and stood silently looking down at her.

Seconds later, as the sun sank beyond the verdant Galilean hills and the Great Sea beyond, the woman suddenly lay quietly. Her right palm slowly wiped the moisture from her forehead. Tentatively, she moved her feet off the bed. Her face showed surprise as she rose and stood, facing Jesus.

In a house lit only with an oil lamp, Jesus was surrounded by eight or nine sick or infirm people. Wordlessly, Jesus reached out his hands and gently touched a middle-aged balding man, whose beard was soaked with the agony within his body.

The man opened his eyes and looked up at Jesus. The man's hands came up in an involuntary movement, hesitated in midair, then carefully settled on his distended abdomen. The hands kept going down. So did the abdomen. When the stomach was flat, the man let out a delighted cry.

Jesus turned away, reaching out healing hands to the next person. Moments later, to the same look of surprise and delight, Jesus moved on, touching each aching, hurting, suffering body and leaving each free of pain.

Early one morning at the pretty lake called Gennesaret, a century of Roman soldiers marched along the lakeshore road. They passed an assembly of Jews at the water's edge.

Jesus stood on the quayside, his hands raised to emphasize a point. Close by, a couple of fishing boats were lying prow-to against the stony shore.

"Once there were two men who went up to the Temple to pray," Jesus began. "One was a Pharisee, the other a tax collector. The Pharisee stood by himself and prayed."

Jesus mimicked the Pharisee. "I thank you, God, that I am not greedy, dishonest, or an adulterer like everybody else. I thank you that I am not like that tax collector over there! I fast two days a week and I give you one-tenth of all my income."

Most of the crowd listened motionlessly. Nearby, however, three men worked as they listened. They wore little more than a waistcloth, which left the upper body bare. The garment wrapped tightly around the loins and reaching to the knees, marking them as fishermen. Among them was Simon Peter.

He was powerfully built, with a full head of dark, slightly wavy hair and a beard to match. A hint of premature gray showed in the facial hair. It didn't mean Peter was old; in fact, like all the disciples, he was young. But people aged quickly, and signs of the harsh life usually marked a person early in life. His eyes were bright and alert, missing no detail of his net-mending, while his ears picked up the speaker's story.

Brothers James and John, sons of the well-to-do Zebedee, were also listening. James, the older, was prematurely balding in front. A thin strand of graying hair still clung tenaciously to his forehead. But the gray in his beard was pronounced, although he was still a relatively young man.

His brother, John, had a wide, square forehead with nearly straight black hair. An enormous, totally black moustache covered his upper lip. A heavy beard covered his cheeks and chin with such abundance that his mouth was almost totally lost to sight. John's heavy dark eyebrows gave his grave, tender eyes a steadiness—a steadiness which suggested compassion and dependability.

Jesus' story continued. "But the tax collector stood at a distance and would not even raise his face to heaven, but beat on his breast and said, 'God have pity on me, a sinner!'"

The sons of Zebedee looked up as Jesus hesitated a moment, but Peter's eyes remained firmly on the net, which his strong fingers deftly mended.

"I tell you," Jesus' voice reached the three fishermen again, "the tax collector and not the Pharisee was in the right with God when he went home."

Jesus made an expansive gesture, so his plain, off-white sleeves flared widely, "For everyone who makes himself great will be humbled, and everyone who humbles himself will be made great."

The story ended to mixed reaction of the crowd. The three fishermen stopped their work and looked thoughtfully at Jesus. His eyes locked on Peter's.

For a moment, the two men looked at each other, then Peter's eyes dropped before the steady gaze of the white-robed figure.

Jesus said, "Push the boat out further to the deep water, and you and your partners let down your nets for a catch."

The tall fisherman brushed the wavy dark hair off his forehead with an impulsive and impatient motion. "Master, we worked hard all night long, and caught nothing. . . ."

Peter hesitated; something in Jesus' face persuaded him.

"But," Simon Peter said, sucking in his breath in a sudden decisive movement, "if you say so, I will let down the nets!"

Peter looked toward his partners and called, "James! John!"

Zebedee's sons dropped their nets and hurried to join Jesus and Peter.

The two fishing boats rocked gently on the lake. Simon Peter thoughtfully considered Jesus in the bow of his boat. In the second nearby boat, James abruptly shook his head. His younger brother dipped his head in a short motion of agreement. It all seemed pretty futile; they had obeyed Jesus and let down their nets, but there was no indication of any fish. The three fishermen glanced at one another in quick consent. Impulsively, Peter grabbed his net and began hauling it into the boat. The brothers did the same.

Jesus seemed unconcerned. He sat at the bow of Peter's craft and looked pensively into the pretty blue waters of the lake.

Suddenly, the water between the two boats seemed to come alive. "Look!" Peter exclaimed. "Look!" The other two fishermen let out startled cries, as something caught their eyes under the surface. Their hauling motions ceased. They bent over the gunwales, as the lake suddenly boiled with hundreds of fish.

In moments, the fishermen were straining against the sagging weight of filled nets. Calling advice to one another, the partners heaved and pulled with bulging shoulder and arm muscles against the unusually heavy catch.

Bright fish spilled out of the dripping nets and onto the fishermen's feet. The men laughed as the silvery catch continued to spill into the boats and stack up in flapping heaps to the gunwales.

Jesus' face showed the strain, as he enthusiastically joined Peter, James, and John in their strenuous efforts. But when the last portion of net fell soggily into the boat atop the immense catches, Jesus' face relaxed.

Shouting joyfully to one another and collapsing from their exertion, the men glanced briefly at the three-and four-pound fish with the pale-blue stripes, which streaked horizontally up their flat sides. Then, as realization hit the fishermen, they turned awed eyes toward the white-robed figure of Jesus.

Peter shook his head disbelievingly at the catch in both boats. The decks were buried under the teeming catch. Peter's boat rode low in the water; it was virtually down to the gunwales.

Peter turned his head again, to confirm what he had already seen in his partners' boat. It, too, was so low with the weight of the catch that lake waters slapped gently at the lip of the gunwale.

Peter saw that James and John were exhausted. They had collapsed in joyful fatigue on top of their immense catch.

But Peter turned again to Jesus, approached him with awe, and knelt in front of him.

"Go away from me, Lord! I am a sinful man!"

Jesus, still resting calmly at his place by the mast, said gently: "Don't be afraid; from now on you will be catching men."

CHAPTER TEN

THE STREET in front of a village synagogue was clogged with people. Many were invalids. They sat or lay listlessly beside the mud-brick walls and watched helplessly, as the more healthy people pushed and shoved their way along the dirty, narrow street to the synagogue.

Four bearded men purposefully called, "Make way! Let us through!" The men carried a stretcher of two long poles and an old cloth. A paralyzed man lay on the stretcher. Only his head moved, as his bearers continued their efforts to reach the synagogue door. It was impossible. The crowd, packed tightly together, had no room to give. The stretcher-bearers antagonized some of the men nearest them, who resisted with outthrust elbows.

The stretcher-bearers lost their momentum. They slowed, hesitated, and then stopped.

From his litter, the paralytic called, "Never mind! There'll be another time."

The first bearer was not defeated.. "No!" His eyes sought the tantalizing synagogue, so near, and yet unreachable. "No, no! We'll make it! You'll see!"

A powerfully built Roman soldier was attracted by the hubbub. He shoved his way through with his curved shield in his left hand. He brandished an ugly battle-ax in his right hand. The Jews squeezed together to let him through.

"What's this?" He roughly shoved the last few men aside and stood towering over the four litter-bearers and their helpless cargo. "What's going on here?"

The crowd tried to explain. They pointed at the synagogue. Various ones called out:

"Jesus of Nazareth is healing the sick."

"The power of the Lord is present!"

"These men are trying to get through."

The burly Roman frowned, hefting his ax and menacingly tapping it on the decorated shield.

The man on the stretcher turned his eyes to the bearer nearest his head. "Let's forego this."

The determined man at his right foot ordered, "Be calm! We'll find a way in!"

The soldier glowered at the bearer, but the one nearest the paralytic's left shoulder added his voice to their leader's. "Don't worry! You're in good hands."

Suddenly, he had an idea. "This way!"

He turned with such force that the other three men yielded. They moved away from the soldier, back through the crowd, which parted to let them out with their paralyzed friend.

Soon the four men had climbed to the flat roof of a two-story Jewish home located next to the synagogue. With subdued voices in respect to their proximity to the synagogue, the men urged one another to be careful as they transferred their friend to the synagogue roof. There they carefully lowered him, wiped perspiration from their foreheads, and considered another problem.

"The synagogue always faces toward the Temple," their leader mused, raising his eyes toward the hills, where Jerusalem was hidden. "So he would be standing about . . . there!"

The other men nodded and bent to the synagogue roof. Carefully, they pulled away heavy tiles. They worked quickly and carefully, while the sounds of the crowd outside the synagogue drifted faintly up to their ears.

Inside and below them, the experts in Jewish Law, scribes, Pharisees, and others sat on the stone benches and tried to listen to Jesus. But a distracting sound on the roof slowly fastened every eye on what was happening there.

Simon Peter, James, and John, leaning against the walls near the three synagogue doors, looked up, too.

A broadly grinning bearded face peered through a newly made hole in the ceiling. The head disappeared. More and more tiles were quickly pulled away.

The seated men below began to mutter angrily. Some got to their feet to protest, while others stood curiously. They craned their necks to see more clearly what was happening at the widening roof hole.

Slowly, carefully, the stretcher descended through the hole. Ropes at each corner of the litter were stretched taut as the four men on the roof lowered their paralyzed friend, until the stretcher came to rest right in front of Jesus.

He looked down at the paralyzed man. The audience's chatter abated.

Jesus spoke quietly. "Your sins are forgiven, my friend."

The paralytic's face showed his disappointment. He seemed to be thinking, *I didn't come for* that!

The synagogue's membership reacted in an even more positive way. Various scribes and Pharisees demanded of one another, "Who is this man who speaks such blasphemy?"

A scribe declared, "God is the only one who can forgive sins!"

Jesus' eyes moved across the crowd. The protests died down, as he opened his mouth in rebuke.

"Why do you think such things? Is it easier to say, 'Your sins are forgiven you,' or to say, 'Get up and walk?'"

No one answered.

Jesus continued, "I will prove to you, then, that the Son of Man has authority on earth to forgive sins!"

Jesus lowered his gaze to the paralytic. "I tell you, get up, pick up your bed, and go home!"

The congregation peered over one another's shoulders, as the sick man slowly began to move his right hand. It came up before his face. He looked at it with eyes suddenly flooding with grateful, unbelieving tears.

The man on the stretcher gleefully waggled his fingers. Then he began to cry for joy. He got quickly to his feet.

His four friends dropped through the roof hole and started shouting. Tearfully, exultantly, they pointed at their now-standing friend; then clasped him in mighty bear hugs of pure joy.

"Glory be to God in the highest!" the leader's voice cried. "Praise the Lord!"

The others exclaimed, "A miracle! He's healed! Look at him! He hasn't been able to move a finger, and now...."

The people inside the synagogue filtered out. Jesus followed them. Immediately, he was mobbed by the waiting crowd, who had heard what happened inside moments before.

Simon Peter, James, and John attempted to shield Jesus from the noisy crush. But it was a frantic voice, which smashed through the crowd's babble and brought silence.

"Jesus! Son of Man! I beg you to save my only daughter!"

There was something so urgent, so compelling in the voice back in the crowd that the noises began to die down.

"Sir!" The voice was closer now, more desperate. "Have mercy! She's only twelve years old—and dying! Please! Oh, please! Come with me!"

Few things in life are more compelling than a frantic

parent's pleadings for a child. Jesus seemed to be the exception, however, for he looked at the man, but continued to move along.

The crowd recognized the anguished man as Jairus, a synagogue official. The desperate man ran after Jesus and prostrated himself at his feet.

But the crowd of petitioners was so vast that they swarmed forward, trying to be near Jesus. Their soulful cries rang out with equal entreaty: "Lord, help me!"

"Cure me!" another shouted.

"Teacher! Teacher, I...."

Jesus seemed to be the one calm person in the entire mass of seething humanity. By now, the press of people had become so great that Jesus could not move. The prostrate Jairus still lay at his feet, moaning softly with the terrible hurt for his dying daughter.

But in that incredible crush of hurting, sobbing, and crying humanity, one woman desperately grabbed for his cloak.

She touched it; just touched it. That was all.

Jesus stopped immediately. He scanned the dark, hysterical faces around him. He turned to Peter, whose large figure had managed to stay even with him in the crush.

Jesus asked, "Who touched me?"

There was no reply. The crowd continued to bray pleas for help. Simon Peter, assessing the situation with a fisherman's practical eye, said, "Master, the people are all around you and crowding in on you...."

Jesus interrupted. "Someone touched me, for I knew it when power went out of me."

The woman, in her middle thirties, held out her hand to catch Jesus' attention. Her voice trembled, as she confessed.

"I touched you, Lord. I touched you because I suffered many years from bleeding, and spent all I had on doctors...."

Her faltering voice trailed off.

Jesus said gently, "My daughter, your faith has made you well. Go in peace."

As the woman turned away, a Pharisee pushed his way through to Jairus. He had risen to his knees, his hands clasped tightly, trying to make his fatherly feelings felt by this man who had felt someone touch him in that vast crowd. Yet Jesus somehow seemed unaware of the man before him.

The Pharisee gently touched the kneeling man's shoulder. "Jairus," the Pharisee said quietly, "I'm sorry. Your daughter has died." The father sagged against his informer's knees. The friend said softly, "Don't bother the teacher any longer."

Jesus overheard. He looked down at the father, who had dissolved into the fearsome grief of a parent who had lost a child.

Jesus said, "Don't be afraid; only believe, and she will be well."

Inside Jairus's home, his distraught wife and four women friends sat on low benches placed around the dead little girl's bed. The bereaved mother was inconsolable.

A well-meaning friend patted the mother on her arm.

"God will give you solace. The Lord has not forgotten to be merciful."

Before the mother could reply, the door burst open. Jairus swept through with the urgency of a father on a vital mission. He didn't look back at Jesus, Peter, James, and John, who followed him into the room. Jairus's eyes went to his daughter. She lay lifeless on the low bed.

Jairus burst into tears.

Jesus, standing inside the door flanked by the three disciples, was clearly moved by Jairus' grief.

"Don't cry," Jesus said. "The child is not dead—she is only sleeping."

The women friends seated around the dead girl's bed exchanged embarrassed glances. Then, as the reaction hit them, they began to titter. This grew to scornful laughter.

Jesus ignored them. He walked quickly to the child's side. He took the girl's lifeless hands in his. Slowly, Jesus stepped back, pulling the girl.

"Get up, child!"

Jesus continued to pull on the girl's hands. Before anyone could protest, the girl's feet touched the floor. Her head came up, and her eyes opened.

Suddenly, she was standing upright!

The friends' astonished exclamations seemed lost on Jesus.

"Give her something to eat," he said.

CHAPTER ELEVEN

A BEGGAR WOMAN hesitated upon seeing the customs booth at the city gate. She recognized Levi, the tax collector. For a moment, she hung back, watching the familiar scene. Merchants and travelers argued and haggled with Levi, but invariably they reluctantly paid, before he waved them through.

Every Jewish tax collector was regarded with contempt by his fellow citizens, for the tax collector worked for the Romans. He made his profit by charging more than the conquerors required him to collect.

With a sigh and a quick thought about what she would offer as an excuse, the beggar woman shuffled toward Levi. His dark beard was a little sparse and somewhat shaggy. His hair completely covered his ears. His headcovering was a cloth, secured by a headband made from a twisted piece of cloth. This covered his forehead almost to his eyebrows. It was a forerunner of the keffiyeh and burnoose designed to keep the sun off the wearer's head and neck.

Levi looked up as the beggar approached, smiled slightly, and bowed his head graciously. With a casual wave of his hand, he ushered her by his tollbooth and into the city.

Jesus arrived at the gate, just as the woman flashed a toothless smile of gratitude at Levi.

Jesus was trailed by the cured paralytic, the woman who had touched his cloak, and Jairus's wife and daughter.

Levi recognized the former paralytic, who had been lowered through the synagogue roof. Levi gaped in open-mouthed wonder.

The cured paralytic exclaimed to Levi, "The Teacher! He has forgiven my sins!"

As Levi continued to stare in disbelief at the enraptured speaker, Jairus stepped forward and paid the toll for the entire entourage.

Jesus passed last through the gate, then turned back to Levi. "Follow me."

Wordlessly, obeying a command he could not ignore, Levi left his booth and followed Jesus. Thereafter, Levi was known as Matthew.

Jesus was up long before daybreak. He had left the camp alone and returned, refreshed after a private prayertime. He walked through the camp at sunrise. Children were already playing. Babies cried inside tents. About him, women were praying or quietly talking among themselves.

Peter, James, and John, with Matthew, followed Jesus. He paused on his slow trek through the disciples' camp to extend a hand toward one of the growing band of faithful who followed him. By the time Jesus had reached the far end of the camp, eight other men had joined the procession.

Jesus turned to look thoughtfully at these twelve. Andrew was clean-shaven. Like young men of any period, he was more stylish than older men. The Hellenism of most Jews allowed shorter hair and shaving. As fashionable, Andrew wore a twisted band of red and black cloth around his shoulder-length hair. He had been a follower of John the Baptist. Andrew was a brother to the impetuous, opinionated, outspoken Simon Peter. But Andrew was totally unlike his brother in all ways except one: they had both been fishermen.

Simon the Zealot was also beardless. He, too, wore a plaited headband to keep his hair out of his eyes. His jaw was strong and square, reflecting something of his intense nationalist feelings and zealousness for God.

Philip had encountered Jesus at Bethany beyond the Jordan. Jesus, himself, had invited the resident of Bethsaida on the Sea of Galilee to become a disciple. Philip was retiring and quiet; totally unlike his friend, Peter.

Philip's dark beard was short, almost in the manner of the Romans. Philip hadn't trimmed his beard; he was just one of those young men whose facial growth wasn't ever going to be long.

His black hair tended to curl. It cascaded over his wide forehead to rest slightly to the right, over a brown eye.

Thomas had such an extensive head of curling black hair that it seemed almost unnatural. It sat low on his forehead, like a helmet, and flowed down on either side of clean-shaven cheeks.

James, son of Alphaeus, looked somewhat like James, son of Zebedee. This second James was smaller in stature than any of his companions. He was bearded, but his cheeks and a line of receding hair on his forehead seemed to make him look a little more Roman than Jewish.

Judas, son of James, wore his long, wavy shoulder-length hair tied back with a twisted strip of cloth.

Bartholomew's shorter hair curled in an unruly manner across his head and down his forehead toward the short, youthful beard.

The twelfth disciple also wore a headdress of cloth, held by a twisted band. He had a fierce black beard. He was the little company's treasurer, being entrusted with their common purse. Judas Iscariot was the only Judean in the band of disciples. The others came from Galilee, traditional hotbed of dissent. Judeans tended to look down on their agricultural northern neighbors, as though they were a little more rustic and not as knowledgeable as those who lived closer to Jerusalem.

There was something about Judas's eyes which made people look at him, glance away, and then steal another look. There was no word for the feeling Judas's dark, narrowed eyes gave people. But it was there, just the same; a real unnamable *something* which set him apart.

Jesus looked back at the twelve men. He had chosen

each of them himself. Many other men also followed Jesus, plus several women who supported the disciples' ministry with their means. But the twelve men were those Jesus had personally selected to be closest to him. They had followed him for many reasons—reasons as personal as their own individual hopes and dreams.

Jesus stood for a moment longer, looking at these men who had been fishermen, a tax collector, and other unpretentious occupations.

They had left all and followed him: James and John, sons of Zebedee; brothers Andrew and Peter; Levi or Matthew; beardless Simon the Zealot and Philip; clean-shaven Thomas; James, son of Alphaeus; and Judas, son of James; plus Bartholomew and Judas Iscariot.

Jesus turned and walked out of the camp. The twelve disciples followed

In a meadow, beside a camp, a crowd nucleus was growing larger, as a great flux of men and women streamed in the same direction and swelled the gathering into a vast audience. When they were seated and turned attentively toward Jesus, he began to teach them.

"Happy are you poor; the Kingdom of God is yours! Happy are you who are hungry now...."

The sermon continued as the others hurried to join the listeners. The latecomers arrived with impatient tugs on lead ropes to patient donkeys or ill-tempered camels. A few carts squeaked and rocked precariously on wooden wheels. The general mood of all the audience was joy without boisterousness. They didn't lose their good feelings, even when those already seated shushed them to silence.

Jesus continued his beatitudes, as the audience listened raptly.

"... you will be filled! Happy are you who weep now; you will laugh! Happy are you when people hate you, reject you, insult you, and say that you are evil, all because of the Son of Man!"

Jesus began to move slowly, circulating among his audience.

"Be glad when that happens and dance for joy, because a great reward is kept for you in heaven. For their ancestors did the very same things to the prophets."

The audience showed various reactions to Jesus' words, but he seemed not to notice. He kept moving among them, letting his voice carry a stirring new message to an ancient people.

"But how terrible for you who are rich now; you have had your easy life! How terrible for you who are full now; you will go hungry! How terrible for you who laugh now; you will mourn and weep! How terrible when all people speak well of you; their ancestors said the very same things about the false prophets."

Nearby, in the camp, a woman had been milking a goat, while her small daughter watched. The woman stopped, straining to hear Jesus' words, which carried faintly to her. Her husband arrived and pointed toward Jesus. The woman set her cup on the ground and swept the child into her arms. The family hurried toward the crowd.

Jesus' words continued unbroken. "But I tell you who hear me: Love your enemies, do good to those who hate you, bless those who curse you, and pray for those who mistreat you. If anyone hits you on one cheek, let him hit the other one too; if someone takes your coat, let him have your shirt as well. Give to everyone who asks you for something, and when someone takes what is yours, do not ask for it back."

Jesus paused, looking over the silent audience. "Do for others," he continued, "just what you want them to do for you...."

A change came over the crowd. There was something about Jesus which suddenly made everyone want to touch him. The people began to reach out and touch him, as he moved among them. Those who could not reach him stood, moving forward with outstretched hands.

The disciples pushed their way through the eager hands and surrounded Jesus, trying to form a protective cordon about him.

Jesus didn't allow himself to be interrupted.

"If you love only the people who love you, why should you receive a blessing? Even sinners love those who love them! And if you do good only to those who do good to you, why should you receive a blessing? Even sinners do that."

Other disciples, who followed Jesus but were not among the inner circle of twelve, were moved by their leader's words.

One such disciple, carried away with his exuberance, exclaimed: "He will wash away the sins of man!"

A little girl frowned at the two men. She placed a finger across her lips and whispered, "Shh!"

Jesus continued. "Love your enemies and do good to them; lend and expect nothing back. You will then have a great reward, and you will be sons of the Most High God. For he is good to the ungrateful and the wicked. Be merciful just as your Father is merciful."

The faces turned toward Jesus showed many reactions. Old or young, sick or crippled, lovers and long-married couples were mostly enraptured by Jesus' words. A few Roman soldiers in their red tunics were assigned to prevent Jewish gatherings from creating disturbances. They regarded Jesus with growing suspicion.

Jesus continued unbroken. "Do not judge others, and God will not judge you; do not condemn others, and God will not condemn you; forgive others, and God will forgive you. Give to others, and God will give to you."

An old woman, sitting apart from the crowd, held a ram's horn, so the narrow end would funnel Jesus' words to her failing ears. A small girl repeated Jesus' words into the wide mouth of the horn.

"One blind man cannot lead another one; if he does, both will fall into a ditch."

Jesus paused, seeming to gauge the audience's needs.

"Why do you look at the speck in your brother's eye, but pay no attention to the log in your own eye? How can you say to your brother, 'Please, brother, let me take that speck out of your eye,' yet cannot even see the log in your own eye?"

He was a promise. A promise made to a nation centuries before. A promise of salvation ...redemption. A promise many thought God had broken.

A young girl...Mary was her name...was told by an angel that she would be used by God to fulfill that promise. She would give life to that promise. Jesus.

JESUS

It's not the kind of news you keep to yourself! Excitedly, she hurried off to share her news with her aged aunt, Elizabeth. But Elizabeth had some news of her own. She, too, was going to give birth to a son— John. And this son was to prepare the way for Mary's son, the Savior of the people.

About that time, the Roman government decided they should find out how many people were under their rule in the land of Israel. Mary and her husband-to-be, Joseph, were ordered to travel to Bethlehem, a small city, to report for the census. So Mary, quite far along in her pregnancy, made the long journey. And because it was impossible to find lodgings in the bustling town, she gave birth to Jesus...the promised one...in a dark, damp stable.

Another person received a promise from God: an old man named Simeon. He had been told that he would not die until he had seen his people's Savior. Upon entering the temple one day, he knew that the promise had become a reality. With praise in his heart, Simeon took the baby into his arms.

The un-noticed birth was announced only to a handful of shepherds tending their flocks that night. Perhaps because they would be the only ones to believe the news given to them by angels. Perhaps because only some humble shepherds would understand that God could fulfill His promise in such a humble way.

As the years passed, Elizabeth's son began to realize that he was born with a purpose—to make the people of Israel ready for the appearance of the Messiah. And so John, making his home on a river bank, living off only what the land could provide, began to call men and women to God.

"Turn away from your sins and be baptized, and God will forgive you."

The people didn't know what to think of this tattered man. Some thought he was a raving lunatic. Others asked him if he was the Messiah...the promised one.

"I baptize with water. But one more powerful than I will come, the thongs of whose sandals I am not even worthy to untie. And He will baptize you with the Holy Spirit and with fire."

Quietly, but purposefully, a lone figure stepped out from the crowd, and John was caught by surprise. His pulse quickened as the man joined him in the water.

"Look, the Lamb of God, who takes away the sin of the world."

"Baptize me, John." said the man of promise.

The watching crowds stood in amazement as the heavens opened, and the Spirit, in the form of a snow-white dove, descended and perched on Jesus' shoulder.

"This is my beloved Son whom I love. I am pleased with Him."

For the forty days following this remarkable event at the river Jordan, Jesus traveled the parched desert on foot, where He was tempted and tormented by Satan. It was a time of prayer...of preparation...to the life of purpose that was to follow.

While walking along the water's edge, Jesus spotted some rough fishermen who had readied their nets, and had set sail, only to be met with dismal results. Jesus offered His advice:

"Put into deeper water, and let out your nets for a catch."

Skeptical at first, the fisherman decided to humor this stranger. Imagine their surprise when their nets were filled nearly to the breaking point, and their tiny boat began to sink! Struggling, laughing with delight, fighting the currents and their overloaded nets, the fishermen finally made it back to shore.

"Follow me," Jesus said, "and you will be fishing for men."

For some reason not yet really clear to any of them, they followed Him. Fishermen, tax collectors, political radicals—just about the oddest collection of men that could be gathered together. But Jesus poured His life into these men—His disciples. He taught them many things about His heavenly kingdom...and about His earthly purpose.

"These seeds are like the Word of God. Some are cast along the roadside, some on hard ground, some into the thorns. But only a few seeds fall on good soil, and grow.

Still they had their doubts. But those doubts were erased in the midst of a violent storm. Awakening Jesus from a sound sleep, they begged Him to save them from certain death, should their boat sink in the swelling waters.

A single command calmed their fears:

"Peace be still."

In utter amazement, they asked each other the only question on their minds.

"Who is this? He commands even the wind and water, and they obey Him."

On the opposite shore of the lake, Jesus and His band of followers came upon a man who was possessed by a flood of demons. Recognizing Jesus, the demons begged Him to allow them to enter a herd of pigs. Jesus consented, and ordered them to leave the man.

The demons violently entered the pigs, and they wildly stampeded down a sharp cliff, plunging into the lake below, where they drowned.

Somewhat impressed by the fact that the mad-man was now sane and fully clothed, the herdsmen and townspeople were nonetheless overcome with fear and anger.

"You magician! Leave us! Go away from here and leave us alone."

Curiosity about Jesus spread
across the countryside like
brush-fire, and the people
gathered to find out more
about this man whose very
words and thoughts became
physical realities. Often, Jesus
would teach more than 5,000
people at a time, in a single
place.

With darkness approaching, the disciples began voicing their concern that the people who had gathered on the hill-side to listen to Jesus would have to be sent away hungry. And the only food they could find was a few small loaves of bread and a couple of fish.

Jesus ordered the people to sit down in groups of about 50 each. Then, He placed the loaves and fish in baskets, raised them toward heaven, and blessed them.

After feeding the entire crowd, the disciples were still able to gather up 12 baskets of left-overs.

Naturally, word of what Jesus had done spread quickly!

Though the crowd sought Him out at every opportunity, Jesus still saw the need to spend concentrated time with His closest followers, teaching them truths that would change their world.

"If anyone wants to come with me, he must forget himself, and take up his cross and follow me."

"If you had faith as big as a mustard seed, you could say to this mulberry tree, 'Pull yourself up by the roots, and plant yourself in the sea,' and it would obey you!"

His earthly ministry touched young and old. Children were especially close to His heart.

"Let the little children come to me, for the Kingdom of God belongs to them. Whoever welcomes this child in my name, welcomes me; and whoever welcomes me, welcomes the One who sent me. For he who is the least among all of you is the greatest."

Ten lepers came to Him,
begging for a miracle…a
miracle they each received.
But only one—realizing what
had happened to him—turned
back to thank his Master.

"Son of David, have mercy on
me!" cried a man who was
blind from birth.
"What do you want me to do
for you?"
"Lord, I want to see."

With profound compassion,
Jesus the Promised Son of God
reached out to the poor, the
paralyzed, the deaf, the blind.
And the humble faith of those
who sought His healing touch
was the spark that released His
power...and His love.

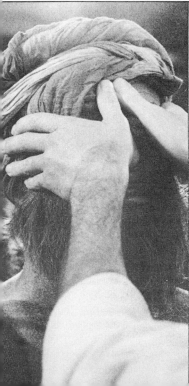

"Receive your sight; your
faith has healed you."

His name was Zacchaeus, and he wasn't too well-liked. You see, he was a tax collector. And a crooked one at that. But he still wanted to see what all this talk was about. Who was this Jesus anyway?

He followed the crowds out to where Jesus was, but because he was rather short, he couldn't even get a glimpse of the Teacher. A tree by the roadside appeared to be the perfect solution to his problem.

When Jesus reached the tree, He stared straight up at the little fellow, and said, "Hurry down, Zacchaeus, for I must stay at your house today."

Zacchaeus scrambled to the ground and warmly received Jesus into his home, much to the dismay of the onlookers who couldn't imagine why Jesus would hang around with such unsavory types.

But that brief visit was enough to completely transform the unscrupulous tax man.

"Listen, I will give half my belongings to the poor, and if I have cheated anyone, I will pay him back four times as much."

"Today salvation has come to
this house. For the Son of
Man came to seek and to save
the lost."

But some of the things He did displeased the religious leaders of the time. Upon discovering that a marketplace had been set up in the temple, Jesus stormed in, overturned the tables, and drove the merchants out into the streets.

Recognizing Jesus as a threat, the leaders began to implement their plans to capture Him.

Many who heard Him teach, and witnessed His miracles were convinced that He was indeed their promised Messiah . . . their Savior. And they freely poured out their praise and gratitude to Him, honoring Him with their songs of "Hosanna." For a brief moment, as He rode a donkey through the pressing crowds, it appeared to everyone that their king was indeed among them.

The perfect plot presented itself through one of the disciples, Judas Iscariot. For a small bag of coins, this disciple-turned-traitor agreed to betray Jesus with a kiss. And under cover of night, leading a small battalion of soldiers, Judas carried out his promise.

The representatives of the Roman government—Pilate and Herod—were too weak-willed to realize that the charges against Jesus were totally false. Eager to please the people, they bowed to the pressures from the council of religious leaders.

When asked pointed questions, Jesus remained silent, refusing to defend himself. He remained silent when mocked and ridiculed. He remained silent when beaten, tortured, clubbed. He remained silent when the bloody barbs of a quickly improvised crown of thorns were jammed into His head. He remained silent because He had to. His humiliation, His suffering, His death, were all a part of God's promise.

Under the back-breaking strain of a dirty, rough-hewn cross, Jesus was led out of the city, past the crowds that had once sung His name in praise, to a hill they called "Golgotha" — "The Place of The Skull."

As His mother watched in agony, Jesus was nailed to the cross He had borne. The pain —as those nails first pierced— is impossible to imagine. But love doesn't come without great cost...

JESUS

For one dreadful moment, as the cross was dropped with a sharp jolt into a hole in the ground, His flesh must have ripped and torn under the strain. How can a mere man, in the face of such excruciating pain say:

"Father forgive them. They don't know what they're doing."

A mere man couldn't.

Even one of the two thieves crucified on either side of Jesus was able to grasp the depth of His love...and the certainty of who He was.

"Remember me, Jesus, when you come as King."

"I promise that today you will be with me in Paradise."

Was it mockery? Or was it sincere? Pilate ordered that a sign reading "The King of the Jews" be nailed to the cross.

In that history-transforming moment when Jesus passed from life to death, a sudden darkness, unlike any darkness the world had ever seen, crept across Calvary. That day, the darkness was pierced by a new light—the brilliant light of salvation.

"Glory be to God. Certainly He was a good man."

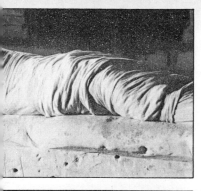

A 24-hour guard was posted outside the borrowed tomb where the body of Jesus was laid...a guard that could keep his followers out. But that's about **all** it could do.

On the third day, a group of women led by Mary Magdalene hurried to the tomb, in hopes of anointing Jesus' body. They were surprised to find that the guards were not there. And the huge stone at the entrance had been rolled away! But nothing could compare with their surprise upon entering the tomb. The grave clothes were empty. Jesus was missing!

"He is not here. He is risen."

The women rushed off to find Peter and the other disciples who were equally dumbfounded by the strange sight of any empty tomb.

Their shock and grief turned to joy, as several times over the next 40 days, Jesus walked and talked with them, and showed them the scars of His love for them.

On a cloudless day, as His followers stood in open-mouthed amazement, Jesus left His earthly home for the Kingdom of His Father.

But He left them with a promise...

"I will come back for you, so that you may be with me where I am."

Cover concept by Bob Screen
Art by Visual Communications/Minneapolis
Photo section written by Steve Gottry
Designed by Dave Gjerness

In the crowd, the man known as Simon the Pharisee sat with a friend.

His companion leaned against Simon's shoulder and asked tentatively, "Do you think he might *be* the Messiah?"

Simon looked back at Jesus and pursed his lips. "In any case, I would like to know this man."

Jesus had stopped. He looked about the audience.

A woman with two small children gave vent to her feelings. She shouted, "How happy is the woman who bore you and nursed you."

Jesus turned to her. "Rather," he said mildly, "how happy are those who hear the word of God—and obey it!"

Jesus lay in exhausted sleep on a hilltop. His head was propped against a rock. The twelve disciples relaxed under a sycamore tree. In the background, the crowd seemed reluctant to leave, as though hopeful Jesus would return and speak again.

Bartholomew pulled off his shirt, moved to Jesus, and gently slipped it under his head.

Miles away, in the great stone fortress of Machaerus, two of John the Baptist's disciples approached the forbidding structure with obvious fear. They explained their purpose to a series of blue-garbed Herodian guards who passed them deep within the vast, ugly structure, until they were deep underground. Finally, at the end of a long, dismal, echoing corridor of rough stones, where the smell of death was strong, they paused before a small combination air hole and window in the damp walls. One disciple called into the tiny opening. "John?"

At first, there was only the scratching of tiny claws scrambling deeper into the dungeon darkness.

John the Baptist's gaunt face appeared in the window. He reached eager fingers through the tight bars and clung to his disciples' hands.

The spokesman said, "We've come with news."

"News?" John's voice echoed hollowly in the semi-darkness.

"About Jesus of Nazareth."

The baptizer listened in silence, as the two visitors updated him on events outside the fortress-prison and across the Jordan in the green hills of Galilee.

The more talkative of the visitors concluded with another story. "As we arrived at the gate of Nain, a funeral procession came out. The dead man was the only son of a widow."

"Yes?" John prompted.

"When Jesus saw her, his heart was filled with compassion. He touched the body and said, 'Young man! Get up, I tell you!'"

The less talkative visitor was too excited not to participate. "Then the dead man sat up and began to talk, and Jesus gave him back to his mother!"

John's eyes reflected the dancing light of the torches held in the corridor. The same question was obviously going through his mind as that which had brought the two disciples to him.

"Do you think," the spokesman asked, "That Jesus is . . . the Messiah?"

John's voice echoed through the dungeon. "Ask him!"

John's disciples were intimidated by the prospect. They exchanged apprehensive glances.

John's eyes shone through the bars. "Say to him, 'Are you the one John said was going to come, or should we expect someone else?'"

The two disciples listened to the baptizer's complete instructions. Then they took their leave, walking out of the ugly fortress-prison, to carry John the Baptist's questions to Jesus.

Chapter Twelve

Meat was a rarity in most Jewish homes, because it was so expensive, but in Simon the Pharisee's kitchen, a large woman servant glazed a large platter of *kibi* with fresh egg yolks. Behind her ample frame, a six-year-old boy and his eight-year-old sister exchanged mischievious glances. The boy reached for some parsley and began making a forest in the chopped meat. His sister suppressed a giggle and joined in the fun.

The servant turned away to attend a boiling cauldron, leaving the freshly glazed *kibi* unguarded. The children choked back giggles and began poking parsley sprigs into the *kibi*.

The servant, preoccupied with her thoughts, picked up the green-topped *kibi* without seeing the decorations. She carried the dish through the doorway into an adjoining room.

Jesus, Simon the Pharisee, his friend, and four other

male guests reclined on couches around a low table. They leaned on their left arms and ate with their right hand from a table laden with platters of lamb, bread, fruit, and jugs of wine.

The children poked their heads through the kitchen doorway and giggled hysterically, as the servant set the platter in front of Simon. She still hadn't seen the "improvements" they had made, but Jesus had. He caught the children's suppressed giggles and smiled warmly at them. Nobody else had noticed the unusual decorations on the *kibi*.

Suddenly, there was a frantic pounding at the outside door. A woman shrieked, "I must see him! I must! Let me in. Oh, please let me in!"

The servant woman waddled to the door, opened it a crack, and tried to slam it shut again. "No. Not you! Get out of here. *Aieeh!* Go!" The children curiously slipped out of the kitchen and peered around the large protective barrier of the servant woman. A male servant hurried up to the door, as the screaming and pounding continued. The host rose quickly and also went to the door. "What is it? What's the matter?"

The male servant, having taken a quick peek around the edge of the door, which couldn't quite be closed against the outside woman's determined pushing, started to reply. But he let out a yelp and jerked his fingers back. The woman wriggled through the door and plunged through the servants and Simon.

"She bit me, Master."

The male servant shook his fingers and turned to give determined pursuit to the intruder, who wore the heavily jeweled hair of a prostitute. She threw herself at Jesus' feet. She lay there, weeping and trembling. Her long hair covered her shoulders and face.

She had once been pretty. That much had been obvious, as she had raced across the room from the door. Her *colobium*, the simple, square-cut garment without sleeves and only a hole for the neck, was unsashed, so the garment had billowed unattractively. Yet that could not hide the fact the young woman had a slender figure.

The host and his servant moved to the weeping woman. Then Simon laid a restraining hand on the male servant's arm. He reconsidered the situation a moment and then rejoined his guests at the table.

The woman servant, clucking disapprovingly, quickly ushered the children back into the kitchen. The male servant folded his arms disapprovingly and stood behind the prostrate woman, ready to forcibly eject her at Simon's signal. But Simon shook his head slightly and grinned knowingly at his male guests. They got the idea and also smiled in appreciation of hidden knowledge, not shared by Jesus.

Jesus thoughtfully looked in silence at the woman. Slowly, her sobbing eased. She raised her head and turned her tear-stained face up to look at him. The coins linked across her forehead reflected the lights. Tears splashed on Jesus' bare feet, since the Jewish custom was to leave dusty sandals outside in the courtyard after washing their feet and entering the house.

By the unsteady light of olive oil-fueled clay lamps resting on small niches built right into the stone walls, the other guests could be seen suppressing grins, as the woman again bent over Jesus' feet. They were now wet with her tears.

She reached into her long, dark tresses and dried Jesus' feet with her hair. Finally she kissed them and sat upright on her knees. She reached for a tiny alabaster vial dangling from her neck on a string.

Simon cupped his right hand and whispered to his nearest dinner companion. "If this man really were a prophet, he would know who this woman is who is touching him; he would know what kind of sinful life she lives!"

Jesus smiled faintly and looked from the woman, who was pouring the vial's fragrant liquid onto his feet.

"Simon, I have something to tell you."

"Yes, Teacher?"

"There were two men who owed money to a moneylender. One owed him five hundred silver coins, and the other one fifty. Neither of them could pay him back, so he cancelled the debts of both. Which one, then, will love him more?"

"I suppose," Simon replied, "it would be the one who was forgiven more."

Jesus replied, "You are right." He turned his eyes toward the woman, who had finished anointing his feet and was again kissing them.

"Do you see this woman?" Jesus asked Simon. The fragrance of perfume filled the room.

When the Pharisee didn't reply to the obvious, Jesus said quietly, "I came into your home, and you gave me no water for my feet, but she has washed my feet with her tears and dried them with her hair.

"You did not welcome me with a kiss, but she has not stopped kissing my feet since she came. You provided no olive oil for my head, but she has covered my feet with perfume. I tell you, then, the great love she has shown proves that her many sins have been forgiven. But whoever has been forgiven little shows only a little love."

Jesus paused after his rebuke. He touched the woman's long tresses with a reassuring hand. "Your sins are forgiven," he told her. "Your faith has saved you; go in peace."

The guests traded smirks.

The woman was delighted. She smiled through her tears, rose to her feet, and began backing away from Jesus. With a quick, beautiful smile, which glowed more brightly because of her tear-filled eyes, she turned and ran joyfully through the doorway.

CHAPTER THIRTEEN

THE ONLY LIGHT in the street filtered faintly through houses near the synagogue. Simon the Zealot sat on the synagogue's steps, facing into the night. It was empty except for the shadowy bulk of two Roman soldiers conversing in hushed tones across the way. They turned and looked suspiciously at Simon. One approached cautiously.

"Who are you?" he demanded brusquely, hefting his spear. "What are you doing here?"

The clean-shaven disciple nervously adjusted his headband, using both hands. "I'm Simon, a disciple of Jesus of Nazareth. I'm waiting for a companion. He's out looking for bread."

The soldier said nothing. He stood with feet braced, the spear point tilting slightly forward and the butt resting on the ground. He was close enough to reach the sitting man with his weapon, but out of reach if Simon carried a hidden weapon.

A Zealot was anybody zealous for the Lord; fanatically religious Jews who naturally wanted the land to be free of Roman or other occupation forces. A Zealot was really a patriot, believing Palestine was a land which belonged to the Lord. There was not yet a Zealot Party which later openly resisted the Romans and led to the Great Revolt in the 60s. This resulted in the destruction of the Temple and Jerusalem itself in A.D. 70. But Simon the Zealot was a Jewish patriot who was zealous for the Lord in the scriptural sense of his time.

Simon the Zealot felt he must say something more. "We arranged to meet here."

The second Roman interrupted. *"Pst!"*

The first soldier turned to see another shadowy figure, who had entered the narrow street.

The first soldier snapped to Simon the Zealot, "Go find another meeting place." He rejoined his comrade. Both watched the shadow of the approaching man, until he stopped.

The soldiers raised their spears and began moving towards him. He was fumbling in the darkness at the door of a house.

"You there!" The first soldier's voice startled the man at the door. He hesitated. The soldiers hurried their pace toward him. The man turned and ran back the way he had come.

The soldiers gave chase and with angry oaths, they rapidly overtook and tackled the man and dragged him, kicking and protesting, back toward Simon. He pressed himself against the synagogue stone facade.

They passed Simon. The man struggled between the two soldiers, crying vainly, "I'm not a Zealot."

The first soldier's voice came through the night. "Why did we find swords in your house?"

"I don't have any swords. I don't know any Zealots. Not one."

The second soldier's voice was fading away but Simon heard him laugh harshly. "You're a liar. We have our spies."

Simon turned the corner, hurried on tiptoes away from the soldiers and their victim and paused to sigh deeply. He said to himself, "Lord, deliver us from oppression."

In daylight, Chuza, Herod Antipas's steward, stood on the courtyard wall and sternly surveyed the throng below. The area was jammed with Jews spiritedly airing their viewpoints.

"This man really is a prophet."

Another cried, "He *is* the Messiah."

A third sneered, "The Messiah will not come from Galilee."

Another voice added, "The Scripture says that the Messiah will be a descendant of King David."

"And will be born in Bethlehem," another voice shouted. "The town where David lived."

On the wall, Chuza shook his head. Those Jews. Didn't they ever agree on anything? And didn't they know that talk of the Messiah was dangerous? In Galilee, Herod, the tetrarch, and Pontius Pilate, the governor down in Judea, wouldn't like that thought. Not at all. They ruled by right of the emperor in Rome, and none of them would take kindly to any threat to their political power. Besides, if it was true that the Jewish Messiah would have religious as well as civil-military power, he would be a tremendous threat to the Jewish priestly hierarchy. Chuza shook his head again. And even his own wife, Joanna, had been fooled. You'd think a woman of such an important man as Herod's steward would know better than to follow the Nazarene. Still, she had always been a woman of strong convictions. . . .

A large crowd of Jews stood in the hot sun, trying to gain admittance to a large cave. It had been extended out with a lean-to of poles covered with tent material. Jesus and some disciples had taken refuge from the day's heat.

John the Baptist's two disciples, still on their mission for him, pushed their way through the milling throng and approached some of Jesus' disciples who blocked the cave's entrance. Simon the Zealot, Judas Iscariot, and Matthew stood under the awning, admitting no one. Simon Peter recognized John the Baptist's disciples and motioned for them to be admitted. He led them into the cool, darkened cave behind the pole and awning entrance.

The three men stood quietly, until their eyes had adjusted to the dim interior. The smell of domestic animals, dry straw, and invisible dust particles of a barn came strongly to their nostrils.

Jesus had been half-asleep against a stack of sweet-smelling hay. He opened his eyes and sat up.

The spokesman for John's two disciples cleared his

throat and nudged his companion forward.

"Ahh . . . John the Baptist sent us to ask if you are the one he said was going to come, or should we expect someone else?"

Jesus didn't reply for a moment. Then he arose and answered, "Go back and tell John what you have seen and heard: the blind can see, the lame can walk." Jesus paused, gazing steadily into his visitors' eyes, then concluded, "How happy are those who have no doubts about me!"

Outside the cave, the crowd stirred with sudden expectancy. The word sped through the crowd. Parents hoisted children to their shoulders. People bobbed up and down, straining for a glimpse. Young girls squealed with delight.

On the courtyard wall, Chuza frowned down at the throng surging toward the cave entrance. Chuza's eyes had caught a familiar figure in the crowd.

His wife, Joanna, was there. She was with Susanna, a fine-looking olive-skinned young woman. The third one, Chuza saw with distaste, was the controversial woman, Mary Magdalene. Chuza didn't believe a word of the story that Jesus had cast seven demons from her. Still, she had been following the Nazarene for some time. Recently, Joanna and Susanna had also joined the inner circle around Jesus, contributing to his ministry from their private resources.

The crowd's cries brought Chuza's attention back to the courtyard. The people were straining to see the cave's entrance. "Who is it?" "Someone's coming out!" "Is it Jesus?"

Their questions were answered when the Nazarene appeared under the pole-supported awning over the entrance. They greeted him by subsiding into respectful silence. He stepped from the canopy's shade and stood where all could see. The disciples flanked him protectively. Jesus opened his mouth and spoke with such volume that everyone could hear.

"Once there was a man who went out to sow grain. As he scattered the seed in the field, some of it fell along the path, where it was stepped on, and the birds ate it up."

Joanna, standing in the shadow of a tall man near the crowd's edge, let her eyes drift upward on the courtyard wall. Her husband stood, spread-legged and with arms folded over his cuirass. He glowered at her, oblivious to all others. Joanna turned her attention back to Jesus. He continued his parable of the seeds.

"Some of it fell on rocky ground, and when the plants sprouted, they dried up because the soil had no moisture. Some of the seed fell among thorn bushes, which grew up with the plants and choked them."

Joanna stole another look at her husband on the wall. Mary Magdalene and Susanna kept their eyes on Jesus. Joanna turned her attention back to him, when she saw her husband's stance and glower had not changed.

"Some seeds," Jesus was concluding, "fell in good soil, the plants grew and bore grain; one hundred grains each."

Jesus paused, raised his arms dramatically and concluded,

"Listen, then, if you have ears."

He slowly lowered his arms and stood looking over the crowd. Someone shouted, "What does this mean?"

Jesus did not answer. He turned and re-entered the barn.

On the wall, Herod's steward angrily shook his head. Those Jews and their parables. Couldn't they ever say anything clearly? And what in the world his wife could see in listening to such riddles was beyond him. But in a way, Chuza was glad for Jesus' riddles: it was impossible to prove he meant anything against Rome.

That night, the cave was impossibly crowded. Jesus sat under the light of a single sputtering oil lamp. He was abstractedly doodling in the sand with his forefinger. Inside the circle of crowding admirers were the usual twelve disciples, plus Mary Magdalene, Susanna, and Joanna. With their eyes, each seemed to be urging the other to ask Jesus a question.

It was the short-bearded Philip who spoke.

"Why do you speak in parables whenever a crowd is near?"

Jesus looked at the young disciple, and then again looked at the symbols he had scrawled in the barn's dirt floor. For a moment, it appeared he was not going to answer. Then he said:

"The knowledge of the secrets of the Kingdom of God has been given to you, but to the rest it comes by means of parables, so that they may look but not see, and listen but not understand. . . ."

His voice trailed off. He again raked the dirt floor with his fingers.

"This," he said, "is what the parable means."

He picked up a handful of sand. "The seed is the word of God."

Jesus scattered some dirt in front of him.

"The seeds that fell along the path stand for those who hear; but the Devil comes and takes the message away from their hearts in order to keep them from believing and being saved."

Jesus scattered more dirt, hitting a piece of field stone which had been carried in.

"The seeds that fell on rocky ground stand for those who hear the message and receive it gladly. But it does not sink deep into them; they believe only for a while, but when the time of testing comes, they fall away."

Jesus threw some dirt toward a corner.

"The seeds that fell among thorn bushes stand for those who hear; but the worries and riches and pleasures of this life crowd in and choke them, and their fruit never ripens."

Jesus dropped the remaining dirt from his hand and raked it with his fingers to blend it into the soil.

"The seeds that fell in good soil stand for those who hear the message and retain it in a good and obedient heart, and they persist until they bear fruit."

Jesus got up, brushed his hands together and moved toward the oil lamp. He lifted it from the rocky ledge and moved past the open cave door.

Outside, in the soft night, Judas Iscariot was speaking with Mary, Jesus' mother, and two young men.

If Jesus saw or recognized them, he gave no

indication. He moved around the circle of crowded listeners in the cave and paused to hold the light above his head.

"No one lights a lamp and covers it with a bowl or puts it under a bed."

Jesus reached higher and set the lamp on a wall bracket. The flame danced unsteadily for a moment, then righted itself and glowed brightly.

"Instead," Jesus said, "he puts it on the lampstand, so that people will see the light as they come in."

He paused, looking into each listener's eyes. "Whatever is hidden away will be brought out into the open, and whatever is covered up will be found and brought to light." Judas Iscariot entered the cave and waited for Jesus to finish. "Be careful, then, how you listen," Jesus said, "because whoever has something will be given more, but whoever has nothing will have taken away from him even the little he thinks he has."

Jesus sat down again. The crowd began to discuss his remarks. Judas raised his voice from the door.

"Teacher, your mother and brothers are standing outside and want to see you."

Jesus looked up and answered, "My mother and brothers are those who hear the word of God and obey it."

One night John the Baptist's disciples returned to Machaerus with the answer Jesus had given them. The Baptizer heard the report through the narrow, dark airhole. He nodded thoughtfully. John seemed satisfied. The two disciples completed their visit and left the dismal, echoing dungeon lit only by the fitful wall torches.

As the men walked across the darkened courtyard toward the outer gate, the sounds of drunken laughter and music beat on their ears.

At the gate, one of John's disciples asked the guard, "Somebody having a feast?"

The guard smirked. "A birthday party for His Excellency, Herod the tetrarch. I sure wish I had the duty inside that hall tonight, instead of out here."

"Oh?"

The guard lowered his voice. "His wife's daughter by her first husband is going to dance for the guests."

"Herodias?" the disciple asked.

"No, her daughter, Salome. She's about seventeen, I hear, maybe nineteen. Anyway, it's said that when she dances, no man can deny her anything."

The guard opened the gate and let John's two disciples out into the night. One turned to the other and asked thoughtfully, "I wonder what the dancer will ask of the tetrarch tonight?"

A few days later, everyone heard what she had asked that night. In a moment of drunken exuberance, Herod Antipas offered his stepdaughter anything she wanted, in appreciation for her dancing. The girl had gone to her mother, the scheming Herodias, who had originally gotten John the Baptist imprisoned.

Her mother sent Salome back to Herod the tetrarch with a grisly request. "Give me here and now the head of John the Baptist on a plate!"

Antipas had been saddened, but, because he had sworn in front of his guests to give the girl anything she wanted, the tetrarch had no choice. He gave orders that Salome's wish be granted.

John the Baptist was beheaded in prison and his head brought to the girl. She took it to her mother.

John the Baptist's disciples came, claimed his body, and buried it. Then they went to tell Jesus. He went off by himself alone, as he often did.

When he returned, he took up his ministry with great conviction.

CHAPTER FOURTEEN

THE FISHING BOAT was caught in one of those sudden, violent squalls which can hit the Sea of Galilee. It was daytime, but the torrents of rain were blown so hard by the wind that it appeared almost night. The fishing craft was taking water and threatening to capsize. All twelve disciples were bailing furiously, while a couple of sailors dashed about securing everything loose. Their frightened cries and shouts of advice were shredded by the screeching wind.

A desperate Peter dashed to where Jesus was asleep on a long pillow of rushes. The fisherman bent quickly over Jesus and shook him.

"Master! Master! We're about to die!"

Jesus opened his eyes and saw the despair in Peter's wet, fatigued face. Jesus remained calm.

At the edge of a bluff overlooking the lake, a filthy, naked madman stood giggling in the rain. His uncut, black hair had matted with rivulets of water into his equally untidy, full beard. Except for his eyes, barely visible through the soaking locks, and his cheeks and nose, he seemed to be entirely hair. Even his bony chest and arms were hairy. He watched the floundering fishing boat and danced excitedly, giggling delightedly as he ignored the driving rain.

Jesus arose and stood on the boat's deck with Peter. Absolute pandemonium reigned. The frightened disciples yelled at each other to bail faster. At the same time, they struggled to keep from being swept overboard by the wild waves and squalling winds.

Jesus walked calmly to the bow and raised his arms in reproach to the wind and waves. Almost at once, the squall seemed to stop. It did not pass; it simply dissolved, to be replaced by calm seas and a shaft of brilliant sunshine.

Jesus turned to the twelve and asked mildly, "Where is your faith?"

The sky was still a heavy blue-gray over the bluff where the Gerasene demoniac had stopped his dancing and giggling. He leaned forward over the bluff, peering through his dripping forehead hair at the fishing boat now being made secure to the shore. As the disciples and Jesus slowly climbed ashore, the naked madman darted down a rocky, slippery path to emerge behind some limestone outcroppings by the shore.

Suddenly, the demoniac stopped dead still, staring at Jesus.

Jesus calmly returned the look, then detached himself from the disciples. The madman seized a large rock in his left hand and wordlessly threatened the white-robed figure above him.

Jesus did not flinch.

The hand holding the rock faltered. The tensed biceps relaxed, and the rock plopped wetly to the ground.

The demoniac spoke with difficulty. His words seemed to have a strange, three-part disharmony, as though more than one person were speaking, although the words were distinctly understood.

"Jesus! Son of the Most High God! What do you want with me? I beg you, don't punish me!"

Jesus said with severity, "What is your name?"

There was no response.

Jesus pointed at the man, whose body reacted with violent, involuntary jerking.

The strange mixture of many voices improperly blended as one replied, "My name is 'Mob.' Lord, we beg you—do not send us into the abyss!"

Jesus' pointing finger did not waver. But he raised his eyes and saw two herdsmen with their swine, moving along the top of the bluff where the madman had originally been.

The madman also saw the hogs. The man pointed toward them, and the weird conglomeration of voices pleaded, "Let us enter the herd of swine!"

Jesus raised his hand toward the hogs. Suddenly the whole herd stamped toward the precipice. Their startled herders ran to head them off, but they started leaping over the brink in a stream of squealing, grunting animals that vanished into the lake.

The herdsmen were desperately shouting. "Stop! Stop! Come back!" But it was useless. In a few moments, every animal had thrown itself into the water.

The madman sat calmly in the mud by the lake. His eyes had lost their madness. He looked disbelieving at his naked torso and self-consciously crossed his thin, hairy arms across his body.

Andrew, the youthful, beardless disciple, quickly stripped off his outer tunic and gave it to the man. He slipped into it with Andrew's help.

The swine herdsmen vented their loss on Jesus by waving their goads and yelling, "Magician!" They ran threateningly toward Jesus, calling more angrily. "You! Magician! Leave us! Go from this place!"

Jesus did not move. Andrew helped the demoniac to his feet.

The sight of the madman, now calm and obviously in his right mind, seemed to frighten the swine herdsmen more than the "magician" they had accused of sorcery. Suddenly, the two herdsmen turned and ran down the hill out of sight.

The demoniac turned to Jesus and spoke in a normal voice.

"Let me go with you."

Jesus said quietly, "Go back home and tell what God has done for you."

The man obeyed. Soon everyone in the area had heard what had happened to him. The crowds which had followed Jesus grew ever larger.

Five thousand people sat on a grassy hill at sunset. At the crowd's edge, Joanna poured from a wineskin on a donkey's back, filling drinking vessels.

She called, "Andrew? Mary Magdalene? Did you find some food?"

The youthful disciple and Mary came up to Chuza's wife. They were accompanied by a small boy bearing two wicker baskets on a yoke about his sturdy shoulders.

Andrew explained, "There's a boy here who has five loaves of barley bread and two fish."

Joanna was obviously disappointed. "So little!" She looked over the crowd. "And they are so many!"

Most of the disciples were close enough to hear this latest report. They had already searched fruitlessly for provisions. Impulsively, Simon Peter turned away. He walked resolutely to a rock, where Jesus was sitting.

"Send the people away, so that they can go to the villages and farms around here and find food and lodging, because this is a lonely place."

Jesus looked steadily up at the fisherman and shook his head. "You yourselves give them something to eat."

Peter's face showed dismay. But Mary Magdalene intervened. She indicated the boy's yoke.

"All we have are five loaves and two fish!"

Jesus didn't say anything.

Andrew expressed an incredible thought: "Do you want us to go and buy food for this *whole* crowd?"

Mary Magdalene and all the disciples stared unbelievingly at Jesus.

He said, "Make the people sit down in groups of about fifty each."

The disciples shook their heads but went off to do his bidding.

Jesus stood and smiled and spoke kindly to the boy with the loaves and fishes. Jesus took the yoke from the boy's shoulder. Jesus sat down and indicated the lad should do the same.

As he did, Mary Magdalene and Joanna stared at the two baskets. There were barley loaves spilling out over the top of the basket. Fishes seemed to flow out of the other ba_ket.

With delighted cries, the women began transferring an unending supply of food from the boy's yoke to other baskets.

Jesus stopped them momentarily with the ancient expression of gratitude: "Blessed art Thou, O Lord, our God. . . ."

The two disciples moved throughout the crowd, now neatly grouped in companies, distributing the food. Each disciple was yoked with baskets brimming with fish and bread which they handed to the people.

They raised their united voices to echo the blessing: ". . . King of the Universe, who bringeth forth bread from the earth."

At dusk, on the same grassy hillside now empty of all except the inner circle, Jesus watched, as the disciples brought in the last of twelve surplus baskets of food.

Jesus turned to Simon Peter. "Who do the crowds say I am?"

The fisherman replied, "Some say that you are John the Baptist. Others say you are Elijah, while others say that one of the prophets of long ago has come back to life."

Jesus looked into the gathering dusk and fixed Peter with unwavering eyes. "What about you? Who do you say I am?"

Simon Peter looked steadily into Jesus' eyes. The fisherman's gaze continued, taking in Jesus' face and features, as though analyzing every aspect to confirm Peter's thoughts. But the disciple did not speak for a moment. He let the silence build with his own inner-probing thoughts. Finally, with the quiet conviction of a man who is absolutely sure of what he's saying, and the meaning of that declaration, Peter spoke.

"You are God's Messiah."

It was an answer from the heart. It was also a messianic declaration, which could get a man arrested by the Romans as plotting against them, since the Messiah was to be the Jewish leader. Simon's remark amounted to a civil threat.

Jesus firmly told Peter, "You shall tell no man of this!"

A soft, melancholy tone came into Jesus' next words. "The Son of Man must suffer much and be rejected by the elders, the chief priests, and the teachers of the Law. He will be put to death, but three days later, he will be raised to life."

Not Peter, nor the other disciples, nor any of the women understood what Jesus meant. They looked at one another. But there was something about Jesus' face which made them think it was not the time to ask for a clarification.

Later, about twenty people, including the twelve apostles and other disciples, were gathered around campfires. Some had already stretched out under their tunics or blankets. Mary Magdalene and Joanna sat beside Susanna, who was softly singing in a pure, lyrical voice. Thomas accompanied her on a harp, as she sang from the Nineteenth Psalm.

> How clearly the sky reveals God's glory! How plainly it shows what he has done. Each day announces it to the following day; each night repeats it to the next.
>
> No speech or words are used, no sound is heard; yet their voice goes out to all the world and is heard to the ends of the earth....

The psalmist's words floated gently over the group. Some sat and listened peacefully. Others listened from where they were stretched out, half-asleep. Matthew lay on his back, contemplating the stars spangled across the night sky. The former tax collector rolled over to speak with Simon the Zealot sitting alongside.

"Someone should go ahead to the villages and make everything ready for him."

Simon the Zealot thought a moment before asking, "Us?"

Matthew grinned, "Why not? Will you come?"

The nationalist said fervently, "Most willingly! Tomorrow we'll speak to the Rabbi."

Matthew grinned broadly and clasped Simon the Zealot's hand.

Susanna's song continued.

..God made a home in the sky for the sun. It
comes out in the morning like a happy bridegroom,
like an athlete eager to run a race.

It starts at one end of the sky and goes across to
the other. Nothing can hide from its heat.

Jesus sat listening to the song, while three or four
unfamiliar disciples who'd joined the apostles crowded
around him. One said, "I will follow you, sir; but first let
me go and say good-bye to my family."

Jesus looked through the campfire's glow and said,
"Anyone who starts to plow, and then keeps looking
back is of no use for the Kingdom of God."

Jesus moved his head to include the other new
disciples. "If anyone wants to come with me, he must
forget himself, take up his cross every day, and follow
me.

"For whoever wants to save his own life will lose it,
but whoever loses his life for my sake will save it. Will a
person gain anything if he wins the whole world but
himself is lost or defeated? Of course not!"

"If a person is ashamed of me and my teaching, the
Son of Man will be ashamed of him when he comes in
his glory and in the glory of the Father and of the holy
angels."

Jesus paused, then added, "I assure you that there are
some here who will not die until they have seen the
kingdom of God."

A few days later, a crowd of about a hundred people
stood waiting for Jesus to finish talking with Matthew

and Simon the Zealot.

"Take nothing with you for the trip," Jesus told the twelve apostles. "No walking stick, no beggar's bag, no food, no money; not even an extra shirt."

Jesus swallowed, then raised his right hand in command. "Go! I am sending you like lambs among wolves. Whoever listens to you, listens to me. Whoever rejects you, rejects me; and whoever rejects me rejects the one who sent me."

On the other side of the hundred waiting people, a young man was exorcising a very beautiful, young and demon-possessed girl.

"Come out! Leave her! In the name of Jesus, I order you—come out of this woman!"

The girl trembled with her ordeal. The young man emphasized his commands with stiff, forceful motions of his arms and hands.

John, son of Zebedee and brother of James the fisherman, pushed his way through the bystanders. Jesus had called James and John "Sons of Thunder" for their quick displays of temper. John's temperament showed, as he shouted at the young man.

"Stop! Stop this at once!"

The young exorcist, intent on his mission, ignored the fiery apostle. "Get out in the name of the Son of Man."

John reported to Jesus a few minutes later. The Nazarene was approaching the waiting crowd. Matthew and Simon the Zealot were leaving on their mission. John hurried up to Jesus with a self-satisfied announcement.

"Master, we saw a man driving out demons in your name, and we told him to stop, because he doesn't belong to our group."

There was gentle rebuke in Jesus' reply. "Do not try to stop him, because whoever is not against you is for you."

Peter, James and John were with Jesus one night on a stark hilltop. The apostles had built a small campfire to keep warm, as they slept. They were stretched out in their tunics, while Jesus prayed alone on the hillcrest.

A twig snapped, jerking Peter's eyes open. Still half-asleep, the fisherman turned toward Jesus. "Master? Rabbi?"

Peter blinked. He sat up and rubbed his eyes, stretching his mouth wide in a yawn, then flexing his shoulders. "Master?"

Peter hunted Jesus with his eyes. Suddenly, a look of pure astonishment froze Peter's face. Without taking his eyes off Jesus, Peter reached out big hands and shook the others awake.

The three apostles stared at the praying figure on the hillcrest. Jesus' simple white robe had turned a shimmering phosphorescent. His face radiated a dazzling white.

As Peter, James, and John remained transfixed, a mist engulfed Jesus. A second later, two men walked out of the mist in a brilliant white. One wore a shaggy goatskin mantle; the other was old and gray-bearded. The three astonished disciples knew without a doubt these startling figures were Moses and Elijah.

Peter's impulsiveness overcame his surprise. He came falteringly toward the three: Jesus, the lawgiver from Sinai, and the prophet who had defied the pagan Jezebel centuries before. The brothers trailed Peter.

As the three fishermen cautiously approached, the figures of Moses and Elijah began to fade. In a moment, they were gone. The mist remained.

Peter couldn't stand there and say nothing. It was totally against his nature. He burst out, "Master, how good it is that we are here! We will make three tents, one for you, one for Moses and one for Elijah!"

James reached a restraining hand to Peter and whispered, "What are you saying?"

A mist's density thickened so rapidly that James cried out in fear. "Master! What can we do?"

A voice seemed to come from all directions. It was a deep, rich bass with magnificent overtones of authority.

"This is my Son, whom I have chosen—listen to him!"

The mist vanished as mysteriously as it had come. Moses and Elijah were gone. Jesus was again in his normal state, with his plain, homespun robe of ordinary white.

Peter, James, and John were overwhelmed. They threw themselves face down at Jesus' feet.

In that moment, a turning point was reached in the lives of all four men. Jesus was ready to begin his final journey and an end, which not one of the disciples would have guessed.

CHAPTER FIFTEEN

IT WAS AN INFORMAL scene by a small waterfall. Some of the apostles were bathing their hands. Others washed their clothes. Others prayed, picked wild fruit, or reclined in the sun, eyes closed.

Jesus sat by a small pool below the waterfall, cooling his feet in the water. Andrew approached, drying his hair with the bottom of his loose tunic. "Teacher," the beardless youth said, "when I was with John the Baptist, he taught us how to pray."

Jesus raised his eyes to the first one of the twelve disciples he had called. But Jesus said nothing, waiting for the disciple to finish his thought.

Andrew glanced around at the others, then urged, "Teach us to pray, just as John taught his disciples."

Slowly, Jesus raised his feet from the pool and rubbed them partially dry with his hands. Then he washed his hands in the pool and stood up. Every disciple was now looking at him.

Without formally acknowledging Andrew's request, Jesus began, "When you pray, say this: 'Father: May your holy name be honored.'"

Jesus paused momentarily, making sure all the apostles were attentive. "'May your Kingdom come.'"

Again he paused. "'Give us day by day the food we need.'"

His eyes skimmed the disciples. "'Forgive us our sins, for we forgive everyone who does us wrong.'"

Jesus' brown eyes flickered over the disciples before adding the closing words of his prayer:

"'And do not bring us to hard testing.'"

He got up and began to walk downstream. Andrew and a couple of other disciples followed. Jesus walked awhile and then turned to face the disciples. Jesus raised his voice.

"Would any of you who are fathers give your son a snake when he asks for a fish? As bad as you are, you know how to give good things to your children. How much more, then, will the Father in heaven give the Holy Spirit to those who ask him!"

Some time later, with the same disciples, Jesus walked in a meadow resplendent with wild flowers. The men moved toward a grove of balsam trees. An adjoining wheatfield had attracted a number of crows.

Jesus turned to the disciples. "I tell you, life is much more important than food, and the body is more important than clothes." Jesus pointed to the birds. "Look at the crows."

The disciples' eyes followed Jesus' pointing hands. He continued, "They don't plant seeds, or gather a harvest. God feeds them!" He turned to the disciples and assured them, "You are worth so much more than birds!"

The group walked in silence to the shade of the balsam tree. These grew well in the land, which some called Palestine. The word *Palestine* first appeared in print from the writings of the Greek historian, Herodotus, who had lived four centuries before.

Jesus resumed his thoughts aloud. "Can any of you live a bit longer by worrying about it?"

The uniform shaking of heads caused Jesus to nod briefly in satisfaction.

"If you can't manage even such a small thing, why worry about the other things?"

He waved a hand toward the wildflowers which bloomed so briefly in the land of their fathers. "Look how the wild flowers grow. They don't work or make clothes for themselves. But I tell you," Jesus said with emphasis, gazing at his followers, "that not even King Solomon with all his wealth had clothes as beautiful as one of these flowers."

Jesus reached down and gently touched a lily. "It is God," he continued, "who clothes the wild grass. Wouldn't he be all the more sure to clothe you?"

His eyes moved questioningly across the apostles, who nodded in agreement.

Andrew seemed to feel an inadequacy. "Make our faith greater," he said.

Jesus glanced around, until he saw a plant which had

grown so large it provided a resting place for some large birds. "If you had faith as big as a mustard seed," he explained, "you could say to this mulberry tree, 'Pull yourself up by the roots and plant yourself in the sea...'" Jesus glanced toward the west, where the Great Sea stretched toward Greece and Rome, out of sight beyond the hills, "and it would obey you!"

Jesus sat in the midday sun by the well near a town square eating with a tiny cluster of prostitutes, tax collectors and other outcasts. He took a bite of melon, glanced at two small boys with a mongrel dog, sitting close by, and turned to his audience.

"What is the Kingdom of God like?"

His question caused the listeners to lower their wine or stop chewing. When everyone was focused on him, Jesus answered his own question.

"It is like this. A man takes a mustard seed and plants it in his field. The plant grows and becomes a tree. The birds make their nests in its branches."

A leader of the synagogue passed. His long dark eyebrows arched in surprise at the company Jesus was keeping. Jesus ignored him.

One of the listening prostitutes raised her hand and covered one side of her mouth. She jerked her head slightly toward Jesus and whispered to another prostitute, "I'm not sure what he's talking about, but I like his face!"

The second woman nodded but didn't reply, as the synagogue leader approached Jesus.

"Why do you eat and drink with tax collectors and...other outcasts?"

There were immediate self-righteous reactions from the group. There was mixed embarrassment, indignation, and anger. One made a face and silently mimicked the man's words.

Jesus explained, "People who are well do not need a doctor, but only those who are sick." He looked deeply into the synagogue leader's eyes and concluded, "I have not come to call respectable people to repent, but outcasts."

The prostitutes and tax collectors studied Jesus in thoughtful silence. He had not condemned them. He had stated a fact. None of them was offended.

The synagogue leader sniffed in distaste and walked rapidly away. The first prostitute wrinkled her nose in distain after the retreating figure.

The taller of the boys patted his dog absently. "Tell us again about the Kingdom," he urged like a child who didn't want a story to end. "Is there anything else?"

Jesus turned soft brown eyes on the boy but didn't immediately reply.

The first prostitute asked in a small voice, "Sir, will just a few people be saved?"

Jesus patted the boy affectionately on the head, then took a deep breath. He looked at the woman.

"Do your best to go in through the narrow door, because many people will surely try to go in but will not be able."

His meaning was clearly lost on his small audience.

They looked at one another to confirm that none understood. But they were affable, liking this man who sat with them without embarrassment and genuinely seemed to care about them. Even the small boy managed a grin, as everyone smiled and nodded as though they had understood Jesus' meaning. But it was something each would have to think about, later.

Jesus stood bare-headed in a synagogue. There was no requirement to cover his head. The use of prayer shawls had not begun. Jesus faced the congregation from the reader's position. Among those who sat on the three sides of the room were some tax collectors, who had listened to him talk about going through the narrow door. They listened attentively, but the synagogue leader, who had challenged Jesus earlier, leaned against his neighbor and shielded his mouth behind a cupped hand.

"This man welcomes outcasts—and even eats with them!"

The neighbor critically whispered back, "He is just as we have heard."

Jesus, his back to the three synagogue entrances, began to speak.

"There was once a man who had two sons. The younger one said to him, 'Father, give me my share of the property now.'

"So the man divided his property between his two sons. After a few days, the younger son sold his part of the property and left home with the money."

The listening men displayed various expressions. Some were bored. One was dozing. One was listening intently, as were the women shielded behind the screen toward the back of the synagogue.

Jesus' voice continued with his story. One listener could imagine how it had been with the son.

The son had entered a bawdy house. The room was filled with noise and music. There were signs of heavy drinks, gambling, and prostitution. The young man, very drunk, managed a wry smile as a dancer undulated sensuously toward him. She circled him invitingly. The young man fumbled for his leather purse and held it up. The dancer didn't even smile, as she grabbed the money. She stopped dancing and held out her hands. The young man took them and walked out the back door with the girl.

Jesus' voice brought the synagogue listener back to the present.

"He went to a country far away, where he wasted his money in reckless living. He spent everything he had. Then a severe famine spread over that country."

Jesus' story continued. "And he was left without a thing. So he went to work for one of the citizens of that country, who sent him out to his farm to take care of the pigs. The young man wished he could fill himself with the bean pods the pigs ate, but no one gave him anything to eat.

"At last he came to his senses and said, 'All my father's hired workers have more than they can eat, and here I am about to starve. I will get up and go to my father and say, 'Father, I have sinned against God and against you. I am no longer fit to be called your son. Treat me as one of your hired workers. . . .'"

Jesus continued, "So he got up and started back to his father. He was still a long way from his home when his father saw him; his heart was filled with pity, he ran, threw his arms around his son, and kissed him.

"'Father,' the son said, 'I have sinned against God and against you.'"

"But the father called to his servants, 'Hurry! Bring the best robe and put it on him! Put a ring on his finger and shoes on his feet. Then go and get the prize calf and kill it. Let's celebrate with a feast! For this son of mine was dead, but now he is alive; he was lost, but now he has been found.'"

Jesus continued, "In the meantime, the older son was out in the field. On his way back, when he came close to the house, he heard music and dancing. So he called one of the servants and asked him, 'What's going on?'

"'Your brother has come back home,' the servant answered, 'and your father has killed the prize calf because he got him back safe and sound.'"

The synagogue listener could see the house where the feast was being prepared. Smoke rose from the courtyard. Music and merriment drifted on the wind. The father's other son came angrily in from the fields. He saw the excitement, the musicians, and the scurrying servants.

The older brother's anger deepened, as he approached the courtyard. He saw meat roasting on a spit, wine flowing, and music being made with enthusiasm.

The younger brother was well dressed and clean. The father beamed with happiness, until the servant who'd spoken to the older brother approached him and whispered in his ear. The father looked where his oldest son had stopped, arms on hips and a face black with seething emotions."

Jesus' words wove the scene for the synagogue listeners, as he explained, "The older brother was so angry that he would not go into the house, so his father came out and begged him to come in.

"But he spoke back to his father. 'Look, all these years I have worked for you like a slave, and I have never disobeyed orders! What have you given me?'"

The story had soaked through the mind of the man dozing in the synagogue. He opened his eyes sheepishly to see if anyone had noticed him. No one had. Even the bored man was now leaning forward from his stone bench at the side synagogue wall. He was drinking in Jesus' recounting of how the older son's angry tirade had continued to his patiently listening father.

"'Not even a goat for me to have feast with my friends! But this son of yours wasted all your property on prostitutes, and when he comes back home, you kill the prize calf for him!'

"The father had been silent. Now he spoke, gently, and in deep emotion. 'My son, you are always here with me, and everything I have is yours.'

"'But we had to celebrate and be happy, because your brother was dead, but now he is alive; he was lost, but now he has been found.'"

The story ended. Jesus' audience slowly leaned back, thinking.

Jesus did not look at them, but left the speaker's stand and exited the synagogue. He left each listener to think through the story of the prodigal son.

CHAPTER SIXTEEN

SIMON THE ZEALOT and Matthew had entered a small village. They stood in a tiny square preaching to a group of a dozen or more old women and young children. On the outskirts of their small audience, a boy led a straw-ladened donkey past without even glancing at the speakers. A middle-aged woman waved her hands to drive some chickens down from her doorstep. Some men passed carrying hoes across their shoulders.

But not everyone was indifferent to the two apostles. Six veiled figures, heavily robed, inconspicuously approached from different directions. They converged on the meeting and stood quietly listening to Matthew.

"The Rabbi tells us, 'A healthy tree does not bear bad fruit, nor does a poor tree bear good fruit. Every tree is known by the fruit it bears. A good person brings good out of the treasure of good things in his heart; a bad person brings bad out of his treasure of bad things. For the mouth speaks what the heart is full of.' "

Matthew concluded his quotation. Simon the Zealot opened his mouth to speak, but one of the veiled figures called out.

"Teachers!"

The women and children turned around to see who was interrupting. Matthew and Simon the Zealot waited for the veiled figure to continue.

"Some of our fellows say you have power to cure diseases," one said.

Simon the Zealot answered, "In the name of the Christ, and by the grace of God, we are healers."

Another veiled figure chimed in, "We beg you to heal us!"

The two speakers were joined by the other four veiled figures in a unanimous movement. They dropped their ragged robes and lifted veils to show their faces.

There was instant and collective drawing back by bystanders and passersby. Victims of leprosy and other diseases were very common, but little was known about how the diseases were spread, so nobody wanted to be close to such people.

"Lepers! Lepers!"

Only the two disciples remained surrounded by the hideously deformed intruders. From a safe distance, angry voices were explaining, "These two men brought lepers into the square! Aiieegh!"

Matthew and Simon the Zealot showed a momentary uncertainty. By the Law of Moses, these lepers were to stay outside the camp, calling, "Unclean! Unclean!" to anyone who came near.

Leprosy had deformed the six men's fingers and caused the forward digits to rot and fall off. Their faces were masses of open, putrid sores, except for the tips of their noses; those were gone.

Matthew found his voice. "Come closer."

The horribly deformed men shuffled forward. Matthew and Simon the Zealot exchanged looks, swallowed hard and then, slowly, deliberately, reached their hands toward the two men nearest them.

Instantly, the horrifying facial deformities vanished. The twisted, stubby hands and fingers were restored to naturalness. As unbelieving cries of surprise and joy erupted from the two former lepers' mouths, Simon the Zealot and Matthew healed the other four men.

But the townspeople were too far away to see. In blind fury, they returned with hands full of rocks and pieces of sun-dried house bricks. The furiously cursing, shouting townspeople released their missiles with vicious force.

The now-cured lepers cried out in surprise and pain as the rocks and bricks struck them. Instinctively, they raised their hands to shield their faces. In a moment, new wounds flowed with fresh blood.

Matthew and Simon the Zealot cried out, "Wait! Stop! Look at these men! They're cured! They're no longer lepers!"

The crowd didn't hear a word. They picked up new missiles and hurled them so hard that the six lepers went down, yelling in pain and fright.

The frenzied crowd seized stocks and began beating the helpless figures, which writhed on the ground, hands protectively clutched over their heads, legs drawn up tightly towards their abdomens. Their cries were lost in the furious shrieks of their attackers.

Matthew and Simon the Zealot, bleeding and in pain from the same unreasoning assault, turned and ran. A volley of whistling stones urged them on.

When they had outdistanced the crowd, the apostles collapsed against a couple of olive trees. Simon the Zealot had an ugly bruise over his right eye. He was bleeding from a score of wounds. Both Matthew's cheeks were cut and bloody. He had bruises and lacerations over much of his body. He examined himself carefully, then asked Simon the Zealot.

"You all right?"

"I hurt," he panted, checking himself over. "But nothing serious. Just disappointed."

Matthew nodded. Both men looked back toward the village. Slowly, Matthew rose and began to stamp his feet on the ground, shaking the dust from his sandals.

Simon the Zealot imitated his fellow disciple, remembering Jesus' injunctions about villages and people who would not receive their message.

Simon was still breathless, but he called out to the distant hostiles, "Even the dust from your town that sticks to our feet we wipe off against you!

"But remember that the Kingdom of God has come near you! I assure you that on the Judgment Day, God will show more mercy to Sodom than to this town!"

Not every place was as unreceptive as the town which had driven Matthew and Simon the Zealot out while doing good. Later, the two disciples strode jubilantly through the countryside, returning for a meeting with Jesus.

Matthew was incredulous. "Even the demons obeyed us when we gave them a command in Jesus' name."

"The Master said not to be glad because evil spirits obey you; rather be glad because your name is written in heaven," Simon the Zealot reminded Matthew.

Jesus stood again in the same synagogue where some had been critical a short time before. From his position in front of the three entrances behind him, Jesus was exhorting the congregation seated before him. Two open doors were behind him on either side. The women were behind the screen in the rear.

"Do not be afraid, little flock, for your Father is pleased to give you the Kingdom!"

The men were more attentive than before. Jesus' reputation was growing, and so was the size of his audience.

"Sell all your belongings and give the money to the poor. Provide for yourselves purses that don't wear out and save your riches in heaven, where they will never decrease, because no thief can get to them, and no moth can destroy them...."

He faltered, as he sensed someone entering one of the three entrances behind him. The congregation's collective attention went to the latecomer. Jesus twisted his head enough to see that it was a hunchback woman.

She headed for the women's gallery in back.

The woman hesitated; had the Teacher really motioned her to come to him—here? Jesus had turned back to the audience before him. He resumed his thought.

"... For your heart will always be where your riches are."

Jesus turned to the hunchback woman. She wore a simple, loosely woven head covering. Her dark, almost mauve-colored tunic could not hide the ugly lump which had deformed her shoulders and bent her head forward. She made a move as though to leave, but Jesus smiled and reached both hands toward her.

His plain white robe with the wide, open sleeves rustled softly, as he placed both hands by the woman's ears, beyond her cheekbones.

Quietly, Jesus said, "Woman, you are free from your sickness!"

His hands moved to the deformity. The woman began to cry. Then, still sobbing, she began to straighten up. In surprise, she reached her left hand backward over her shoulder.

Jesus' hands dropped to his side.

The woman felt gingerly with her fingers. Her deformity was gone!

Her look of surprise changed to delight. As she stood tall and straight, her sobs turned to laughter. She cried out with joy, using both hands to assure herself that she was no longer a hunchback.

The synagogue congregation exploded in exclamations. Women behind the curtain peeked cautiously around to see what was going on.

The woman impulsively threw her arms around Jesus' neck and tearfully smothered him with grateful kisses.

The synagogue leader leaped indignantly to his feet and hurried toward Jesus to protest. The man's words were lost in the woman's cries.

"Praise the Lord! Eighteen years! God bless you, Rabbi!"

The synagogue leader interrupted. "There are six days in which we should work," he declared with deep feeling to the woman, "so come during those days and be healed, but not on the Sabbath!"

Jesus impaled the man with a sharp look, then did the same to some congregational men, who were pressing forward, nodding in agreement with their leader.

"You hypocrites!" Jesus' words slashed through the protestors with such power that they halted uncertainly. "Any one of you would untie his ox or his donkey from the stall and take it out to give it water on the Sabbath."

He gestured toward the woman. "Now here is this descendant of Abraham whom Satan has kept in bonds for eighteen years; should she not be released on the Sabbath?"

There were further rumbles of discontent. Various men waved indignant arms and cried out. "That is sinful! Sinful! A distortion of the Law!"

One dubious man frowned and demanded, "How

could a sinner perform such miracles?"

Another shouted, "He is the Messiah!"

There was a jumble of discord and support. Some shouted in favor of Jesus and some against.

Jesus smiled at the joyful woman.

He had made enemies this Sabbath, but Jesus clearly showed he was confident he had done what was right.

But some of the malcontents gathered in tight little groups afterward and debated what should be done with this Jesus who was, in reality, challenging the established authority of the Jewish religious rulers.

"Something has to be done!" one aged man cried.

"Yes," a chorus agreed, "but what?"

The synagogue leader was thoughtful. "I don't know. But there are those who will know."

CHAPTER SEVENTEEN

JESUS HAD the calm, apparently-unconcerned appearance of a man who has faced his fate with godly acceptance. He seemed unruffled about the rumors of opposition building up against him. He had resolutely turned his face toward Jerusalem, where the highest religious and political figures in the land were discussing with increasing intensity what to do about Jesus' challenge to their authority.

He was on the road to Jericho about dusk one night. His eyes took in the usual sights. Two goods-ladened merchants' carts creaked by. A train of heavily ladened donkeys and about thirty weary pedestrians were hiking toward the famous city in the background. It was here, centuries before, that Joshua had picked up the burden the late Moses had surrendered to him. Joshua had circled the famed double walls of Jericho, and the Lord God, who had brought the people out of Egyptian bondage, caused the walls to crumble. The Israelites had taken Jericho and gone on to conquer the land of Canaan, promised long ago to Abraham, Isaac, and Jacob.

A merchant with rich clothes approached Jesus, as he trudged along. He spoke a little pompously.

"Good Teacher, what must I do to receive eternal life?"

Jesus asked sharply, "Why do you call me good? No one is good except God alone."

The merchant fingered his richly adorned robe and lost some of his bravado.

Jesus' tone softened. "You know the commandments: 'Do not commit adultery; do not commit murder; do not accuse anyone falsely; respect your father and your mother.'"

It was a statement which further deflated the merchant's self-assuredness. He lowered his eyes and murmured.

"Ever since I was young, I have obeyed all those commandments."

Jesus nodded in understanding of the merchant's obedience to the ancient laws.

"There is still one thing you need to do," he told the merchant in a quiet, firm voice.

The man's eyes came up to Jesus, and he waited expectantly.

Jesus told him, "Sell all you have and give the money to the poor, and you will have riches in heaven; then come and follow me."

The merchant blinked rapidly, as the impact of

Jesus' instructions soaked painfully into him. Jesus sat down on the back of a cart, as it passed with two merchants driving. A couple of camels passed, heading the opposite way. Simon Peter and Judas Iscariot walked up and stayed alongside the cart, as it continued to rumble along.

Visibly shaken, the merchant found his voice. "But ..." he swept his wide, richly decorated cloak sleeves to include his friends, "we're merchants! Wealth. ..."

Jesus shook his head softly and raised his voice so all could hear. "How hard it is for rich people to enter the Kingdom of God! It is much harder for a rich person to enter the Kingdom of God than ..." he hesitated, looked around, and saw a tall, ungainly camel lurching by. "... than for a camel to go through the eye of a needle."

A second merchant asked a sincere question. "Who, then, can be saved?"

Jesus told him, "What is impossible for man is possible for God."

Simon Peter seemed to feel he should explain something that Jesus had perhaps overlooked.

"Look! We have left our homes to follow you."

Jesus had once healed Simon Peter's mother-in-law of a raging fever. The fisherman had left his wife behind to follow Jesus. The other disciples had also made personal sacrifices.

Their leader nodded to Simon Peter and then included Judas Iscariot in his reply.

"Yes, and I assure you that anyone who leaves home or wife or brothers or parents or children for the sake of the Kingdom of God will receive much more in this present age and eternal life in the age to come."

The merchant asked, "Exactly when will this be— God's Kingdom?" It was a fair question, for it was known the Kingdom would be established. But when?

The Teacher shifted his eyes to the second merchant. "The Kingdom of God does not come in such a way as to be seen. No one will say, 'Look, here it is!' or 'There it is!'; because the Kingdom of God is within you."

There was a long pause. The caravan wound on, passing five Roman crosses erected by the roadside. Two of them supported corpses.

In the custom of the times, both Jewish and Gentile bodies were left suspended on the crosses until a ransom was paid, so the corpse could be removed, or wild animals and birds had devoured them.

Simon Peter and Judas Iscariot moved subconsciously away from the grisly sight. They walked a little closer to Jesus.

He told them, "The time will come when you will wish you could see one of the days of the Son of Man, but you will not see it."

The disciples exchanged glances. Jesus had been using that term more and more: the Son of Man. They knew the expression from the Scriptures, but somehow it seemed to mean something special, something current, to Jesus.

He raised his eyes and arms to the darkening sky. "As the lightning flashes across the sky and lights it up from one end to the other, so will the Son of Man be in his day."

He paused, lowered his arms and eyes and said levelly: "But first he must suffer much and be rejected by the people of this day."

The caravan camped that night beside the rebuilt walls of Jericho. This was the famed City of Palm Trees, and favorite winter home of the Herods. Jericho is about seventeen airline miles from Jerusalem and some thirty-two hundred feet lower than the Temple city. Consequently, Jericho is much warmer when winter rains fall on the higher Judean hills.

A small band of believers had been attracted to Jesus and his apostles. The ever-present Roman soldiers watched the Jews in bored amusement. The legionnaires were aloof from such foolishness as worshiping a God they could not see. The soldiers put more faith in their standards, to which they bowed down in worship, as befitted troops. An invisible God was totally alien to the Romans' thinking.

Jesus was saying, "It is easier for heaven and earth to disappear than for the smallest detail of the Law to be done away with."

A couple of dusty travelers arriving late at the camp, approached the soldiers.

"Who's he?"

The Roman made a sound of disgust. "One more religious fanatic."

The second soldier adjusted his sword in its scabbard. "I would advise you not to get involved."

The travelers nodded and walked on.

The eight or nine people around Jesus were attentive. One asked, "What should we do?"

"What do the Scriptures say? How do you interpret them?"

A voice from the back replied. "'Love the Lord your God with all your heart, with all your soul, with all your strength, and with all your mind'; and 'Love your neighbor as you love yourself.'"

Jesus seemed pleased. "You are right, do this, and you will live."

Another voice called from beyond the campfire, "Who is my neighbor?"

The question brought a sharp exclamation from another man. "Not those soldiers!"

A young man picked up the same thought but phrased it as a question. "What about Caesar?"

It was a dangerous question to ask in front of the soldiers. The audience stirred uneasily.

Jesus waited for the audience to settle down. "There was once a man," he began, "who was going down from Jerusalem to Jericho when robbers attacked him, stripped him, and beat him up, leaving him for dead...."

A listening girl of about eight scooted closer to her mother and made herself comfortable. A story!

Jesus continued his parable, making the small audience see the scene on the steep, narrow, and twisting road, which dropped sharply from Jerusalem down to Jericho. The little girl could see it just as Jesus did.

The victim was a Jew who lay nearly nude and unconscious in the middle of the narrow dirt road.

"It so happened," Jesus continued, "that a priest was going down that road; but when he saw the man, he walked by on the other side...."

The little girl closed her eyes and saw the bearded priest pull his neat, clean clothes about him and hurry on down the hill.

Next, she saw a Levite making his way down the same road. He saw the injured man and carefully approached. The Levite glanced briefly at the victim and saw the extent of his injuries.

Jesus said, "...The Levite looked at the man, and then walked on by on the other side."

The little girl opened her eyes. That poor man! Two of his own countrymen had refused to help him. That wasn't a good story! She liked happy endings!

The little girl perhaps didn't know that, if the priest and Levite had presumed the man was dead, they were forbidden to touch a corpse.

Jesus continued his narrative.

"But a Samaritan who was traveling that way came upon the man."

A *Samaritan!* The little girl made a face. Jews didn't have anything to do with those people who lived between Judea and Galilee! Even though she was very young and didn't know exactly why, she had heard something about the Samaritans being unwelcome to Jews, going back to the time of the Babylonian exile.

Still, the little girl was intrigued by Jesus' story. She kept her eyes on Jesus as he continued.

"...and when he saw him, his heart filled with pity. He went over to him, poured oil and wine on his wounds and bandaged them. Then he put the man on his own animal. . . ."

The little girl could see it happening, even with her eyes open. The Samaritan helped the injured Jew onto his donkey and took him to an inn, where he took care of him.

"The next day," Jesus was saying, "he took out two silver coins and gave them to the innkeeper."

It was a lot of money, the little girl thought: *two silver coins*. She could see the innkeeper reach for them and listen respectfully to the Samaritan when he said, "Take care of him, and when I come back this way, I will pay you whatever else you spend on him.'"

Jesus' story ended. The little girl sighed and closed her eyes. What a good Samaritan!

Jesus said after a pause, "In your opinion, which one of these three acted like a neighbor toward the man attacked by the robbers?"

The little girl's mouth popped open with the answer, "The one who was kind to him!"

Jesus smiled at the little girl. She settled back with a little embarrassment and a good feeling at the same time.

Jesus made an expansive gesture over his audience. "You go then, and do the same."

As the crowd began to leave, Jesus held out his hands toward the little girl. She glanced up at her mother for approval, then smilingly slipped into his embrace.

Only the apostles still remained by the campfire. Jesus' dark eyes were bright as he told them, "Whoever welcomes this child in my name, welcomes me; and whoever welcomes me, also welcomes the one who sent me."

Jesus stopped in that dramatic way he had before concluding, "For he who is least among you all is the greatest."

The next morning, the bright sun drew large numbers of people into the narrow streets. A rumor had spread through the night that Jesus of Nazareth was in town. While some scoffed at stories of his miracles and teachings which had attracted increasingly larger crowds, most of the people were anxious to see him.

The townspeople pushed and shoved, bobbing their heads to get a better look, or trying to find a place where he was sure to pass. Some residents, figuring that the throngs would be too thick for good viewing, had wisely climbed to the rooftops or stuck their heads out of upper windows.

A couple of enterprising young men approached with a rude ladder. They set it up against a large, leaning sycamore and scurried up the ladder and on into the higher limbs.

At the edge of the seething mass of closely packed humanity, a short, overweight man in long, rich-looking cloak scrambled about in the taller forest of normal-sized people. Zacchaeus was the head tax collector in this important city. As such, he was associated with Romans and so was despised by his own people, the Jews. Still he had made a comfortable fortune.

However, his conscience was bothering him somewhat, for his tax collecting methods for the Romans were not above reproach.

Even though he was an important man in an important city, nobody seemed to notice the little man's desperate efforts to find a good place on the street where Jesus would pass. Panting with his efforts, Zacchaeus tried to climb the great wall, but it was comically useless.

Suddenly, just as Zacchaeus seemed to have failed at every turn, he spotted the boys' ladder.

Zacchaeus's rotund face lit up. He darted through the crowd and grasped the rough, handmade ladder. A man in keffiyeh and blue tunic obligingly held the ladder, as word raced through the crowd: Jesus was coming!

Zacchaeus's long, rich cloak, with wide, full sleeves made climbing difficult, but he managed it by abandoning his dignity. He hurried up the ladder and sprawled awkwardly on a large branch. It slanted to the left at a forty-five degree angle in the direction Jesus would come. There Zacchaeus perched, a little precariously but proudly, with the high stone walls of Jericho rising some twenty feet straight up behind him.

The excited crowd surged forward, pushing and shoving to get near Jesus. They shouted and pleaded their many needs, wants, and desires. The little tax collector looked down on the man in the white robe who approached with slow, thoughtful mien.

Just before the crowd reached the sycamore, a blind man moved slowly along the immense fieldstone walls beyond Zacchaeus. The beggar sensed the coming mob and instinctively stretched his ragged frame against the wall. He cocked his head to listen better. He clutched his bowl with the desperation of one who knows he must not lose his only means of livelihood.

Zacchaeus barely noticed the blind beggar's plight. The tax collector watched the people stream past ahead of Jesus, who was nearing the blind man. The beggar groped with his free hand for any passing garment. He snagged a robe on his outstretched hand. The robe's owner stopped and impatiently tugged to free his garment.

The blind man asked, "What's happening? What's going on?"

The man jerked his robe free and ran off, calling over his shoulder, "Jesus of Nazareth is passing by."

Immediately, the blind man clamped his bowl under his left arm and felt for his stick. He grasped it firmly in both hands and shoved himself to his feet. He swept the stick in front of him to detect obstacles. But the heedless crowd swept upon the blind man and spun him along, away from Jesus.

Desperately, turning white, dead eyes toward the place he guessed Jesus to be, the beggar shouted: "Jesus! Son of David! Have mercy on me!"

Jesus caught the cry and stopped. The crowd parted respectfully, as Jesus looked toward the continuing calls, "Jesus! Son of David! Mercy! Mercy!"

The blind man, sensing something in the quieting of the crowd, which had stopped moving around him, yelled his loudest. "Jesus! Jesus of Nazareth!"

Jesus asked quietly, "What do you want me to do for you?"

The beggar flinched at Jesus' nearness. The man had been shouting, when Jesus was right beside him. But this was no time to think of what had been done.

"Sir," the beggar exclaimed earnestly, "I want to see again!"

Jesus answered almost casually, "Then see! Your faith has made you well."

The crowd, which had pressed close around the two, saw it happen: one moment, the scraggly-bearded, blind beggar's eyes had been opaque; almost white, without any center. Some of those watching had known the man for years, and that was the way his eyes were. Then, in the time it took the man to blink in surprise at Jesus' words, the eyes were brown-centered and normal appearing. The opacity was gone.

"I can see!"

The first exclamation was almost breathless.

That was evident from the way he quit cocking his head to one side to listen better; instead he glanced quickly from one spectator to another. His face registered the surprise and delight.

"I can seeee!"

The second shriek of joy was followed by a wild, abandoned throwing up of his bare arms with the ragged sleeves. Then the man's eyes met Jesus.

The beggar dropped to his knees and burst into tears. He embraced Jesus' feet in sobbing joy.

The crowd was visibly stirred. They began praising God.

Jesus slowly released himself from the man and continued on his way. The formerly blind man scrambled to his feet. He instinctively clutched after Jesus' cloak in the way he had done for years. Suddenly realizing that he needn't hold on anymore, the man straightened and followed Jesus, wiping tears from his cheeks and eyes with the back of a dirty hand.

Zacchaeus had seen the entire episode from his precarious perch in the sycamore tree. It was true what they said about Jesus! He could heal a man's physical ailments; could he also help people like Zacchaeus, whose problems didn't show?

Jesus raised his calm eyes to the sycamore tree, under which he was passing. He stifled a smile at sight of the short, corpulent tax collector, beaming happily from the tree top and clutching the limb with a fervent respect for the distance he would fall, if he slipped.

"Zacchaeus!"

The Teacher's use of his name startled the tax collector. He almost lost his grip.

"Hurry down, Zacchaeus," Jesus called again, "because I must stay in your house today."

"*My* house?"

The tax collector's gulped question was drowned in the crowd's instant and unfavorable reaction. A moment before, they had praised God when Jesus healed the blind man. Now a murmur of discontent took the place of praise.

"That's the tax collector! The *chief* tax collector!"

Another rumbled, "Jesus is going to the home of a sinner. Why couldn't he come to *my* house?"

But Zacchaeus was so anxious to get down that he didn't care about the crowd's disapproval. He slid precariously fast down the limb and ladder, tearing his rich clothes and getting burns on his knees and fingers, but he didn't mind. The Teacher was going to be his guest that night!

Zacchaeus's house was large and well lit with many oil lamps. He beamed with pride from his place at the head of the low table. The twelve disciples and Jesus reclined around the table, where the remains of food and wine were evident.

On an impulse, Zacchaeus shoved his portly body away from the table and onto his jewel-sandaled feet. Here was an opportunity to show himself off as a good man. Zacchaeus turned to the wall near the table. He pulled aside a large wall hanging, stood on tiptoe, and removed a stone from its place. The short man probed with his fingers, removed a bag, and turned back to his guests.

"Listen, Sir! I will give half my belongings to the poor, and if I have cheated anyone, I will pay him back four times as much."

Zacchaeus walked to the door, handed the loose stone from the wall to a man, and began pouring out money to the poor from the bag. The people waiting at the rich man's house eagerly reached for the coins.

The twelve couldn't suppress grins. Jesus smiled after their vanished host, before turning soberly to his followers.

"Salvation has come to this house today. For this man

is also a descendant of Abraham."

Jesus paused momentarily and then said something that seemed unrelated. "The Son of Man came to seek and to save the lost."

The disciples settled down in anticipation of a momentous announcement. A moment ago, they had been chuckling with Jesus; now something in his manner warned them to pay close attention.

"Listen," Jesus began so softly that all twelve men automatically leaned forward around the table to hear better. "We are going to Jerusalem, where everything the prophets wrote about the Son of Man will come true."

There was such total silence that even the soft sound of the burning lamps would be heard in the room. "He will be handed over to the Gentiles who will mock him."

That made no sense to the disciples. They had secretly been growing excited about what would happen when they got to Jerusalem. There were rumors that Jesus would announce himself as the Messiah. Some apostles privately expected to benefit personally. James and John, the sons of Zebedee, had asked a special favor. "When you sit on your throne in the glorious Kingdom, we want you to let us sit with you, one at your right and one at your left." Jesus had replied that he did not have the right to choose who would sit next to him; that was God's choice alone.

Still, it wasn't a good idea to hear such things as Jesus was saying. Peter the impetuous started to protest.

But Jesus didn't allow an interruption. He concluded, "They will whip him, and kill him. But three days later, he will rise to life."

The disciples exchanged glances. Obviously, not one understood what Jesus meant. But they were afraid to ask him.

CHAPTER EIGHTEEN

THE LITTLE COMPANY finished the long, steep climb from Jericho and topped the Mount of Olives at twilight. The disciples were excited, as they neared Jerusalem, for they long expected the Kingdom of God was to appear immediately.

Jesus walked ahead of them and stood at the summit. His face was somber. Deep emotions worked behind his dark eyes. He peered through the green leaves, which seemed touched with silver, and let his gaze wander over the panoramic view of Jerusalem. It was separated from the Mount of Olives by the Kidron Valley. Yet even from distance, Jesus could see the evening torches being lighted. The ancient city where David had first ruled a united monarchy centuries ago was twinkling peacefully.

"If you only knew today," Jesus said aloud to the

city, "what is needed for peace!"

His emotion was so deep that Jesus' bearded face worked momentarily before he could continue.

"The time will come when your enemies will surround you with barricades, blockade you, and close in on you from every side."

Tears came, slipping ever faster from Jesus' eyes as he continued his prophecy.

"They will completely destroy you and the people within your walls; because you did not recognize the time when God came to save you!"

He turned away, brushing the tears from his cheeks. He negotiated a short, steep descent to where Philip and Bartholomew waited on the hillside overlooking the tiny village of Bethpage and Bethany. An enormous crowd of disciples milled about.

In the dusk, the curly-haired Bartholomew and the darkly-bearded Philip noticed that Jesus had been weeping, but they were unsure of what to say. They waited for him to speak.

"Go to the village there ahead of you. As you go in you will find a colt tied up that has never been ridden. Untie it and bring it here. If someone asks you why are you untying it, tell them that the master needs it."

Darkness had engulfed the land by the time Bartholomew and Philip had descended from the Mount of Olives and entered the hamlet. It clung like a determined bug to the hillside outside of Jerusalem. The two apostles looked around uncertainly. No one was in the narrow, crooked street, which linked the dozen or so houses which made up the entire hamlet.

The disciples walked around the side of one of the

houses and stopped. Philip pointed through the deepening shadows.

"Look. There."

Two donkeys were tethered to a feedtrough beside the mud-brick house. The little beasts shuffled nervously, as the two men approached. ——

Bartholomew mused, "The one that has never been ridden...." He pointed. "The little one?"

Glancing around a little nervously, the men began untying the colt. The other donkey let out a raucous bray.

A man opened the door and stepped out into the night. "Why are you untying it?" he demanded.

The disciples hesitated. Philip remembered Jesus' instructions and replied.

"The Master needs it."

The owner reflected a moment. "God's will be done."

He watched them lead the young animal away.

In the morning, the disciples followed Jesus down the Mount of Olives where a crowd had gathered, and more people were streaming across the two high roads spanning the Kidron Valley. The brilliantly sunny day was making the Temple sparkle with a majesty that had made men declare it was the most beautiful building on earth.

The rumors had swept through Jerusalem that this was to be *the* day. All the signs pointed to the fact Jesus would do what the majority of Jews thought the Messiah would do: enter Jerusalem in triumph and proclaim the beginning of his Kingdom.

Those who had already arrived encompassed Jesus

and the twelve apostles with an excited, jubilant expectancy. Everyone tried to see exactly what was going on, for it would be a time to remember.

Philip and Bartholomew, feeling a certain pride in their special involvement, threw their own cloaks across the donkey's back. Simon Peter helped their leader to mount.

The significance of that simple act sent a whisper of delight through the throng. Just like in the days of David, when the king or his son had their own donkeys!

As Jesus' mount began to move, the crowd parted before him, as the Red Sea had done for their ancestors. In a few steps, the donkey and his rider had flowed into an area which seemed alive with sound and movement.

As the donkey passed, the crowd closed in tightly and followed, feeling a rising sense of excitement. The feeling of momentous events about to happen engulfed everyone.

Suddenly, Mary Magdalene slipped through the crowd farther down the hill. She hurried up the path, which had opened before Jesus and his mount. The woman from whom Jesus had cast seven demons whipped off her shawl. She bent and quickly spread it in the donkey's path.

Other women followed suit.

A glad shout greeted her action. Other women jerked their shawls from their shoulders and spread them ahead of the donkey's tiny, neat hooves. Men shrugged off their cloaks and spread them in the path. Some enterprising younger men, anticipating Jesus' triumphal entry into Jerusalem, had earlier scrambled up trees and broke palm fronds. These were joyously waved from both sides of the trail where Jesus rode. The disciples bustled importantly alongside Jesus and the donkey.

Somewhere in the excited crowd an ancient cry was raised:

"Hosanna!"

The Greek transliteration of the Hebrew word had once been a supplication. It had evolved into a joyful exclamation in processions at the centuries-old Feast of Tabernacles. The waving of branches had been reserved for the climactic seventh day of the feast. But those moving with Jesus toward Jerusalem meant it in a new and mightier way. Naturally, this would bring attention. It wasn't long in coming. Two priests pushed angrily through the mass of humanity and confronted Jesus. He recognized the current high priest, Joseph Caiaphas, and his father-in-law, Annas, who no longer held the title, but still held the honor as titular head of the Jews' religious community.

"Jesus!" Annas called, puffing slightly with his age and the effort of hurrying. "Jesus. . . ."

He didn't have the breath to continue. His son-in-law raised his voice.

"Teacher! Command your disciples to be quiet!"

Jesus looked at the men who held office by dispensation of the hated Roman conquerors. The crowd instantly subsided into an expectant hush. Here was the confrontation they could tell their sons about!

When Jesus replied, his words were so low and calm that only those nearby caught them.

"I tell you that if they keep quiet, the stones themselves will start shouting!".

The crowd acclaimed Jesus' words. The priests tried to protest again. The crowd's cries drowned them out. The procession passed them. Priests crossed the Kidron Valley on an arch-supported viaduct and entered Jerusalem through the Golden Gate on the east side of the thirty-five acres which housed the Temple.

Inside the gate, Jesus dismounted and moved deliberately toward the Temple grounds. He was bypassed by the running, shoving, shouting men who streamed into the women's gallery in front of the Temples towering, majestic facade. These people wanted to see what happened when Jesus got inside the Temple.

Gracefully curved stairs flanked by stately Corinthian columns marked the way up to the Nicanor Gate, which Jesus entered to the Temple grounds. Beyond the gate was the area where the animals were sacrificed, by the Altar of Burnt Offerings. Just beyond that was the Holy Place. That, in turn, was separated from the Holy of Holies by a veil.

The crowd and disciples seemed to expect Jesus to be near that most sacred spot, where they expected to hear him make the proclamation, for which they had waited so long.

Instead, Jesus turned to his left and walked south into the Court of the Gentiles.

The crowd reacted to this surprising move by progressively quieting down, as they wondered what Jesus was going to do next.

Jesus walked resolutely through the stalls of penned animals and caged birds, waiting to be sacrificed. Jesus made his way up the great stone steps at the back wall. He stopped beside a money-changer's table.

No one was prepared for what happened.

Suddenly, Jesus gripped the money-changer's table and lifted it. Coins clattered to the stone floor. The money-changer shouted and struck at Jesus.

But he wasn't there. He was already moving on, overturning baskets of fruits and vegetables and more money-changers' tables. The merchants yelled and struck at Jesus. He kept moving, shoving over flimsy pens, which allowed frightened sheep to panic in all directions.

The startled crowd scrambled to get out of Jesus' rampage and his furious pursuers. Jesus knocked the larger oxen pens down, the beasts fled into an avalanche of pushing, shoving, screaming humanity, trying to get out of the way. "Stop him!" merchants yelled. "Cut him off!" "Strike him!"

The enraged stall-keepers rushed upon Jesus. But they succeeded only in causing more pens to fall and bird cages to smash open. The air was filled with escaping birds and bleating sheep.

Jesus turned to his pursuers and shouted, "It is written in the Scriptures that God said, 'My Temple will be called a house of prayer!' But you have turned it into a hideout for thieves!"

He overturned another money-changer's table to emphasize his point. Jesus moved on, destroying the business, which was being conducted in the Lord's

Temple. Jesus shoved another table over.

The stall-keepers cried in a ragged chorus of anger and dismay.

"Stop that madman!"

"Look at my merchandise!"

"I'll kill him!"

"Restrain him, somebody!"

"Where's the Temple Guard?"

Panting hard, Jesus stopped and surveyed the pandemonium and disaster around him. The frightened oxen, bawling and plunging in every direction, were scattering what few spectators hadn't retreated to safety. The black-faced sheep darted through the forest of legs. The sheep knocked fleeing men to the pavement, where their fellow humans leaped over them in their own flight to safety.

"Now!" An anguished shopkeeper cried. "Let's get him. Come on! All together."

They tried to rush Jesus, but the fleeing sheep, plunging oxen, and staggering humans delayed most of the attackers.

A few got close enough to rain blows toward Jesus. He nimbly ducked away and vanished into the seething cauldron of humanity.

In a few minutes, the sight of the utter destruction of the Temple's commercial area hit the crowd. Their noise died away to an utter, frightening silence; they saw that Jesus was gone.

But the incident had started a fateful reaction. Jesus had not declared himself the Messiah, as the disciples and many of the people had expected. However, he *had* openly challenged the commercialism of the Temple which provided the high priest with great wealth.

It was also a disturbance which would attract the Romans' attention.

The opposition could no longer ignore Jesus' growing threat.

CHAPTER NINETEEN

ANNAS'S HOUSE reflected the opulence in which he lived But the many lights in ornate wall brackets showed a few Jews in rich robes, sitting with a Roman official drinking over a jug of wine.

Caiaphas strode about the large room in a high state of agitation. "Just think of this! What if he really is...."

He stopped, unable to say the word.

Annas was positive. "He's a carpenter! A carpenter! that's *all* he is!"

The former high priest turned impassionedly to a couple of well-dressed Sadducees. "A Nazarene! You know the Messiah must come from Bethlehem! This man..." Annas waved an arm in the Temple's direction, "... this man is another onerous radical; that's the true nature of the beast! He's sailing too close to the wind, and we are *all* in jeopardy!"

His son-in-law was more calm. "Forget it! Let him

keep talking. He'll end up in a Roman garrison!"

"Are you blind?" Annas demanded. "His following is growing by the day! His popularity already exceeds ours!"

The Roman official made a disgusted sound. He brushed a hand across his clean-shaven cheeks, adjusted his rich toga and observed sarcastically, "That's not difficult."

Seeing the displeasure on Caiaphas's bearded face, the Roman added bluntly, "Don't misunderstand me, high priest! Our ... er ... 'friendship' only extends so far. If this man threatens the peace—I shall look to you."

The naked threat remained, as the Roman strode out, his leather trappings creaking ominously.

A moody silence gripped the remaining men. Caiaphas turned to his father-in-law. "Perhaps you *are* right. It's time we confront this ... this Nazarene."

The next day, Jesus returned with his disciples to the Court of Gentiles. Most of the mess from yesterday had been cleaned up. But the animal pens and bird cages had not been repaired. The area was crowded, but the commercialism was absent. Surprisingly, nobody challenged Jesus.

The disciples walked somberly beside and behind Jesus. Their mood had changed. Yesterday, along with most of Jerusalem, they had expected Jesus to make his announcement that he was the Messiah. Now they weren't sure what to think.

Neither, apparently, were the people in general. The few on hand walked the familiar grounds and quietly debated among themselves about who Jesus really was. Why hadn't he declared himself openly yesterday? They stole dubious glances at him, as he walked along the double rows of columns with flat roofs of the porticoes. These extended to the northwest corner where they joined with the Antonia Fortress. Herod had named it for Antony before that ambitious Roman and the greedy Cleopatra of Egypt had been defeated by Augustus at the Battle of Actium more than half a century before.

Jesus moved leisurely along the first section of porticoes which were more than nine-hundred-feet long. These splendid eastern porticoes or porches, dated back to Solomon's day. In Ezra's time, mass meetings had been held there in what was called "The Street of the House of the Lord."

Jesus watched rich men in their fine glowing robes, depositing gifts of silver and gold into huge stone jars set along the colonnade. These men were different from the money-changers of yesterday, who changed the light Roman coins for the Tyrian shekel, supposedly valued about the same as the holy shekel. These rich men were displaying their generosity, where all could see, placing ornamented cups and silver plates in the recepticles.

A poor-looking woman in black clothing mutely proclaimed her poverty and widowhood, as she moved slowly toward the stone jars. Her gentle face was partially hidden, as she lowered her head to look in her hands. Then she lifted her right hand and dropped two small copper coins in with all the gold and silver. She turned away with a small, self-conscious smile and shuffled across the court toward one of the two southern gates on the Temple grounds.

Jesus watched her go and then said to the disciples, "I tell you that this poor widow has put in more than all the others."

A curious crowd had been watching Jesus from a little way off. They moved quietly forward, as Jesus began to speak. He raised his voice to them.

"For the others offered their gifts from what they had to spare of their riches; but she, poor as she is, gave all that she had to live on."

The widow passed through a gate and out of sight. A buzz of whispered excitement showed the crowd had spotted someone new and interesting.

Jesus raised his eyes. The Roman official from the night before had entered the court with Caiaphas, Annas, and an elder. The high priest stepped important-ly forward and posed a challenge calculated to entrap Jesus.

"Tell us," Caiaphas demanded, "what right do you have to do these things? Who gave you such right?"

The crowd sensed what was happening and settled into a hushed, expectant mass.

Jesus looked around casually and then focused on his questioner. "Now let me ask you a question. Tell me, did John's right to baptize come from God or from man?"

The throng nodded with satisfaction. The Teacher

from Galilee had countered a dangerous move with a good question.

The high priest hesitated. A scribe standing near muttered under his breath, "What shall we say?"

Annas leaned toward his son-in-law to whisper a warning from behind a hand seemingly placed casually over his bearded mouth.

"If we say, 'From God,'" Annas reasoned, "he will say, 'Why, then, did you not believe John?'"

The scribe overheard and mumbled, "But if we say, 'From man,' this whole crowd will stone us, because they are convinced that John was a prophet."

Annas stroked his gray beard before facing Jesus. "Er . . . we don't know where it came from."

Jesus replied, "Neither will I tell you, then, by what right I do these things."

The Roman choked back his laughter. The crowd was more rude. They laughed aloud. Annas and Caiaphas followed the scribe in a quick retreat. The people encircled Jesus with attention and expectancy. He waited until everyone was still.

"There was once a man who planted a vineyard, rented it out to tenants, and then left home for a long time.

"When the time came to gather the grapes, he sent a slave to the tenants to receive from them his share of the harvest.

"But the tenants beat the slave and sent him back without a thing. . . ."

A young man with alert face looked from the crowd

into Jesus' face and visualized the story as the Teacher continued. It was harvesttime, with baskets of fresh grapes spilling over the tops of baskets. A gang of harvesters with sticks and daggers had abandoned the baskets to pursue a young man. He fled for his life through the vines.

"So he sent another slave," Jesus continued, "but the tenants beat him also, treated him shamefully, and sent him back without a thing.

"Then he sent a third slave. The tenants wounded him, too, and threw him out."

The young man listening to Jesus could see the third slave—an older, wiser man, whom his master had thought might command the laborers' respect. But they were as merciless to him as the two other slaves. They were trying to head him off as he cleared the last row of vines and ran for the road. One laborer caught up with the older slave and delivered a heavy blow. The old man's face began bleeding, as he turned and scrambled to his right toward an open field.

"Then," Jesus said, "the owner of the vineyard said, 'What shall I do? I will send my own dear son; surely they will respect him!'"

Jesus' attentive listener could see the owner's son: young, well dressed, and receiving the same brutal treatment as the three slaves. The owner's son retreated under the blows. He stumbled into a ditch, where the harvesters pounced on him before he could regain his feet. Their sticks and clubs rose and fell in a furious onslaught. Finally, panting hard with their exertion, they rose and ran back into the vineyard, leaving the victim for dead.

Jesus explained their reasoning, "When the tenants saw him, they said to one another, 'This is the owner's son. Let's kill him and his property will be ours!'

"So they threw him out of the vineyard and killed him."

The Nazarene met the eye of his attentive young listener and asked, "What, then, will the owner of the vineyard do to the tenants? He will come and kill those men, and turn the vineyard over to other tenants."

The young man cried, "God forbid!"

A neighbor scoffed, "Surely not!"

Jesus asked them, "What, then, does this scripture mean? 'The stone which the builders rejected as worthless turned out to be the most important of all.'"

The listener and his neighbor shrugged and shook their heads. They didn't know. Jesus raised his eyes to the rest of the crowd.

"Everyone who falls on that stone will be cut to pieces," Jesus explained. "And if that stone falls on someone, it will crush him to dust."

The crowd exchanged confused glances. What did it mean?

"Teacher!" A voice broke into the crowd's thoughtful pondering. All eyes turned toward the man, but he was hidden from Jesus' view by the throng.

"Teacher! We know that what you say and teach is right. We know that you pay no attention to man's status, but teach the truth about God's will for man."

The speaker was still not visible to Jesus, but the voice was coming closer as a path opened before him. The last persons stood aside and Jesus recognized a spy of the high priest. He was accompanied by a Roman official.

"Tell us," the spy from Caiaphas challenged, "is it against our Law for us to pay taxes to the Roman emperor, or not?"

The crowd murmured in surprise. It was an entrapment question, asked in front of both Jews, who hated their conquerors who demanded taxes, and the Roman official. He stood, arms folded expectantly across his cuirass.

As one man, the crowd realized that no matter what Jesus replied, he was in trouble. If he spoke against the Jews, the crowd would be angry. If he spoke against the emperor, the Romans could seize Jesus for treason.

Jesus knew exactly what he was going to do, but he was so casual about it that witnesses wondered with a quick catch of breath if the Teacher was aware of the grave peril into which the spy of the high priest Caiaphas was leading him. The Nazarene walked toward Caiaphas's spy and held out his hand.

"Show me a silver coin."

Caiaphas's spy drew his head back in surprise. But he could see no harm in complying with such a simple request. He dug into his girdle, produced a coin, and handed it to Jesus.

"Whose face and name are these on it?"

The spy, fearing a trap, hesitated.

But the crowd knew the answer. Their angry cry rose

in a single word: "The Emperor's!"

Jesus handed the coin back to Caiaphas's spy and said softly, "Well, then, pay to the Emperor what belongs to the Emperor, and pay to God what belongs to God."

The crowd roared with appreciation. Jesus turned his back on the glum-faced spy and the Roman official.

Jesus raised his hands and the crowd hushed immediately.

"Be on your guard against the teachers of the Law, who like to walk around in their long robes and love to be greeted with respect in the marketplace, and make a show of saying long prayers! Their punishment will be all the worse!"

The high priest's spy glowered at Jesus, then hurried away, retreating from the crowd's chuckles. The Roman official trailed the older priest. He shook his head in rueful admiration at the way Jesus had turned the high priests' planned trick back on them. But there was a sobering thought in that incident for the Roman, too. His smile vanished and he frowned. This was no ordinary teacher. The Roman walked to where the elders had been watching under the shaded, flat-roofed eastern portico. Caiaphas was visibly angry.

"Now he's gone too far. And you . . . " the high priest glowered at his father-in-law, "*you* wanted to confront the Nazarene and show that he was nothing but a carpenter!"

Annas was a cagey old man who had long been in power. He knew when to act and when to talk. It was now time to act. He said, "You're right, my son. He's

gone too far! He's challenged our authority time and
time again; or if not us directly, he's challenged the
scribes and Pharisees. Our whole system is in danger
from this man. He must be stopped. And not just for
ourselves; our Roman friend and his companion friends
are also in jeopardy, and he knows it; don't you?"

The Roman was a practical man. He nodded. The
scribe and two priests also nodded slowly in agreement.

CHAPTER TWENTY

JESUS STOOD outside the Temple wall and watched the people go about their business. There was a good cross section of passersby: merchants, soldiers, beggars, priests, women and children, plus their animals.

They were all dwarfed by the great wall of the Temple.

Jesus turned to face the twelve disciples sitting just beyond the wall's edge.

"You will be handed over by your parents, your brothers, your relatives, and your friends, and some of you will be put to death. Everyone will hate you because of me."

The disciples stirred uneasily. What was Jesus saying? What did he mean? Ever since he had made the triumphal entry into Jerusalem and then failed to announce his Messiahship, the disciples had been uneasy. Even after thoughts of the high priests' verbal defeat had brought the hard, sobering realization that a cloud of immense danger was rising over Jesus *and* them. Jesus' last words seemed to portend some terrible calamity slipping upon them, individually and collectively.

"People will faint from fear," Jesus told his small audience with quiet earnestness, "as they wait for what is coming over the whole earth."

He paused, raised his eyes to the great stones of the wall, towering above them, and spoke with a new inflection.

"Then the Son of Man will appear, coming in a cloud with great power and glory. When these things begin to happen, stand up and raise your heads, because your salvation is near."

The twelve listened with fascination and not a little fear, as the authority of Jesus' voice redoubled.

Jesus concluded, "Be on watch and pray always that you will have the strength to go safely through all those things that will happen, and to stand before the Son of Man."

Several Pharisees, scribes and other Sanhedrin members met in the high priest's home. His father-in-law was gesticulating urgently, making a point. The majority nodded in swift agreement, but two men did not.

Caiaphas frowned. "Joseph of Arimathea, why do you hesitate? You're a member of this council. You know the Galilean is clearly a threat to us, and to our nation."

Annas interrupted. "This Nazarene will soon have the Romans down on us unless we act."

The Council was supreme over the Jews in all religious matters. The Romans restricted the right of the Council to execute a capital punishment, but the Council could decide a person was worthy of death. Getting the Romans to carry out the execution was another matter, of course.

Although the Council was a very small body in numbers—compared to the multitudes of Jews they represented—the Council had power to impose its will on the majority. As in any representative form of government, the active minority ruled by silent consent of the majority. The Council was ready to act now against Jesus, and for what the Council members considered good reason.

They were acting out of religious convictions. It was not greed or fear or power, but the good of the whole people they represented. If Jesus continued to openly challenge the religious leaders, to violate their ideas of behavior (such as healing on the Sabbath) then it was clear the Council must stop him. If they did not, Jesus' actions might bring the Romans down on the whole populace. Jesus' continual attraction of such large crowds was likely to make the Romans nervous. He could be seen as a potential political leader who might become seditious and lead an uprising against the occupation forces.

Jesus had to be stopped, the majority of Council members believed, because he was endangering the whole population. That's what the Council members told themselves, believing sincerely that they had to act on a religious principle.

Joseph of Arimathea hesitated to answer Caiaphas's question. He had a secret which, he was not ready to share with these fellow Sanhedrin members. It wasn't that he wanted to keep his secret, the rich merchant told himself severely, it was just that—as yet—he lacked the courage to speak up. That bothered him, and so he hesitated to speak.

Annas's shrewd old eyes tried to find a clue as to what was really behind the merchant's reluctance. But before Annas could phrase a probing question, his son-in-law directed a sharp question to the other dissenter.

"And you, Nicodemus! A Pharisee, a leader in Israel, blessed in all worldly goods, and a member of the Council of Seventy; why do you hold back?"

A cautious, conservative man with a long, curly beard and a receding hairline, Nicodemus hesitated before answering. He also had a secret; at least, he didn't think the high priest and his father-in-law had known that he had once met Jesus by night and had a discussion which impacted Nicodemus's life. (Jesus had told Nicodemus, "No one can see the Kingdom of God unless he is born again."

Nicodemus had asked, "How can a grown man be born again? He certainly cannot enter his mother's womb and be born a second time!"

Jesus had explained that without being born of water and the Spirit, no one could enter the Kingdom of God.)

Nicodemus looked at Caiaphas and ventured a cautious defense of Jesus.

"Our Law does not judge a man unless it first hears from him and knows what he is doing, does it?"

One of the Pharisees sneered. "You are not also from Galilee, are you? Search and see that no prophet arises out of Galilee."

The challenge hung in the emotionally charged air of Caiaphas's home. The other Sanhedrin members glanced around. Only Joseph of Arimathea and Nicodemus did not consent to the plot to kill Jesus.

But neither did these men seem to have courage to fight valiantly for their beliefs. Joseph of Arimathea and Nicodemus exchanged glances from lowered eyes. Embarrassed at their human weaknesses, they immediately broke eye contact. Reluctantly, as the Sanhedrin members waited, Joseph of Arimathea slowly arose. Nicodemus did likewise, sighing deeply and shaking his head at his own lack of courage. He followed Joseph of Arimathea toward the door. Both went out into the night, heads slightly lowered, unwilling even to speak to each other of the mixed fear and beliefs churning in their hearts.

Inside the house, Annas announced grimly, "They're gone. Let's get on with it."

Caiaphas pressed his lips in a tight line, "Are we agreed? Let's see the vote."

Every hand went up. The older priest smiled with satisfaction and nodded to his son-in-law. Caiaphas moved to an inner door, opened it, and admitted Judas Iscariot.

Annas produced a purse from his tunic and weighed some Roman coins into Judas's hands. All the while, the strange, swift eyes of Jesus' only Judean disciple flicked around the room.

"... twenty-nine and thirty," Annas concluded. "As agreed."

Judas made no reply. He put the silver in his purse. His ferretlike eyes swept the room of conspirators, saw the excitement and anticipation, as they realized what was happening. Wordlessly, the most disappointed one of Jesus' twelve apostles faded back into the room from which he had come. The door closed behind him.

The high priest said, "I told him at our earlier meeting, 'Not on the Passover, lest there be a riot.'"

Annas said with satisfaction, "It won't be long now."

The next day, a boy drove a small herd of goats down the narrow streets of Jerusalem. A woman carried firewood on a donkey. Women and girls passed them with pitchers of water on their shoulders. In nearby homes, other women were grinding grain to be made into matzohs for Passover. In close-by pens, men looked over the lambs, which were ready for slaughter.

The city was filling with Jews who had come for the spring celebration, which marked their escape from Egyptian slavery centuries before. Every Jew had known since childhood how God had brought them out of bondage after Pharaoh had repeatedly ignored a series of miracles under Moses. Swiftly, all the first-born of Egypt had died in one night. But the angel of death had passed over the Hebrew slave homes. Only then had the Pharaoh thrust the slaves out of Egypt. The

Hebrews had left in haste. By God's command, the night was annually marked with a meal reminiscent of the first Passover.

"There!" John pointed through the throngs of Passover pedestrians. "A man carrying a jar of water, just as Jesus said we'd find."

Peter and John hurried to meet the man. Some people were staring at him, for carrying water was woman's work.

John spoke to the man. "The Teacher says to you, 'Where is the room where my disciples and I will eat the Passover meal?'"

Wordlessly, the man lowered his water jar and gestured for the disciples to follow him. They came to a two-story, flat-roofed Jewish home and followed the man inside and up to the second story.

That night, with a full moon making Jerusalem's deserted streets bright, Jesus reclined with his disciples in the upper room. Judas Iscariot sat at the end of a long, low table of rough wood planks, his bare feet close to a hatchway ladder.

The other disciples were ranged along the table, reclining on cushions and supporting themselves with their left arms before the table. Jesus sat in the middle, with John next to him on the left, and with Peter beside him.

There was a brooding, sad mood in the room. Jesus looked sadly around the group and then turned his eyes to the table.

In the middle of the platters of food, a small stack of matzoh sat on a piece of linen. An ordinary cup was in front of Jesus, the same as was in front of each man.

The Teacher raised his eyes in the light and explained, "I have wanted so much to eat this Passover meal with you before I suffer."

The disciples exchanged anxious glances, but Jesus continued, "For I tell you, I will never eat it until it is given its full meaning in the Kingdom of God."

He picked up his cup and stood, seeming not to notice the uneasy movements of his twelve followers. Jesus offered the ancient blessing.

"Blessed art Thou, O Lord our God, King of the Universe, Creator of the fruit of the vine."

Jesus passed the cup to his left. John accepted it and held it as the Teacher continued.

"Take this and share it among yourselves. I tell you that from now on I will not drink this wine until the Kingdom of God comes."

The disciples dared not interrupt to ask what was on each of their minds. Instead, each man silently sipped from the cup and passed it on.

Jesus reached for the matzoh.

"Blessed art Thou, O Lord our God, King of the Universe, Who bringeth forth bread from the earth."

He broke the unleavened bread into several pieces and passed it out.

His voice was strong yet barely audible, as he struggled with the emotions so close to his tongue. "This is my body," he said, "which is given for you. Do this in memory of me."

Not a person moved in Jerusalem's street that night. All over the city, bursting with many thousands of visitors who had come for the celebration, Jews had gathered in solemn re-enactment of an age-old ceremony. A child's voice could be heard from each such gathering, each asking the Four Questions, and receiving the traditional answers. The Jews would not forget this night, nor their descendants for thousands of years to come; nor had their ancestors forgotten in the long centuries between Moses and the present moment.

As Jesus paused, a child's voice could be faintly heard from the adjacent house, asking the last of the Four Questions.

Jesus was seated, looking around the table. The meal was over. They had all dipped into the common bowl in the communal custom, and their individual places testified to the untidiness of the practice. But Jesus' place was clean. He had not eaten.

Slowly he stood and passed the cup a second time. "This cup is God's new covenant, sealed with my blood, which is poured out for you."

Peter's impulsive nature obviously was prompting him to rebuke Jesus for this melancholy talk, but before he could speak, Jesus' voice changed.

"But, look! The one who betrays me is here at the table with me!"

The apostles swept the table with searching, frightened eyes. What *was* Jesus talking about? He had behaved so differently, ever since the unexpected cleansing of the Temple a few days before.

Jesus said sadly, "The Son of Man will die as God has decided, but how terrible for that man who betrays him!"

The disciples quickly looked from one to the other, trying to decide which one was being accused. They all muttered at once.

"What? That can't be."

"Who would do such a thing ... ?"

The street was filled with the glow of the full moon. Everyone was home for the Passover meal. Suddenly, a street-level door squeaked open. For a moment, there was no further sound, as the empty streets beckoned to the man at the partially opened door.

Judas Iscariot stepped outside. He glanced nervously around and hurried away. He rounded the corner into the shadows, where even the bright moon could not penetrate.

In the upper room, the eleven apostles had quieted down. Jesus' mysterious and alarming words had been replaced by his usual teaching tone. The men listened, satisfied that Jesus had sent Judas on an errand to give something to the poor, since the Judean kept their common purse.

"The greatest one among you," Jesus was saying, "must be like the youngest, and the leader must be like the servant."

He studied the faces before him, as though seeking an answer to the question he was about to propound. "Who is greater, the one who sits down to eat or the one who serves him? The one who sits down, of course. But I am among you as one who serves."

Again, Jesus examined the men who had walked with him for three years. "You have stayed with me through all my trials, and just as my Father has given me the right to rule, so I will give you the same right. You will eat and drink at my table in my Kingdom, and you will sit on thrones to rule over the twelve tribes of Israel."

Peter was so relieved he couldn't remain quiet any longer. "Then we *are* twelve; there is no traitor!"

Jesus gazed at Peter with keen intensity. "Simon," he said softly, almost sadly, "Simon! Listen! Satan has received permission to test all of you, to separate the good from the bad, as a farmer separates the wheat from the chaff."

Jesus' bearded lips moved with a hidden, controlled emotion which had seeped up into his throat. "But I have prayed for you, Simon, that your faith will not fail. And when you turn back to me, you must strengthen your brothers."

Peter leaped up, anxious to stress his loyalty.

"Lord, I'm ready to go to prison with you, and to die for you!"

Jesus calmly replied, "I tell you, Peter, the rooster will not crow tonight until you have said three times that you do not know me."

Peter started to protest, but conscious that all eyes were on him, he slowly lowered himself to a sitting position.

Jesus waited until the disciples had settled into silence again. His voice had taken on another quality; more emphatic, more powerful than earlier in the evening.

"When I sent you out that time without purse, bag, or shoes, did you lack anything?"

Philip felt Jesus' eyes on him. "Not a thing," he said.

Jesus resumed his instructions. "But now, whoever has a purse or a bag must take it; and whoever does not have a sword must sell his coat and buy one. For I tell you that the scripture which says, 'He shared the fate of criminals,' must come true about me, because what was written about me is coming true."

Simon the Zealot, the patriotic nationalist, leaped to his feet. That was the kind of talk he had expected from the Messiah. The Zealot snatched up two kitchen knives from the table and brandished them in the lamp light.

"Look! Here are two swords, Lord!"

Jesus slowly arose and walked around the table to the ladder sticking up into the room. He turned and saw all of them watching him.

"That is enough," he said, and started down the ladder.

Jesus led his eleven disciples beyond Jerusalem's walls and across the archway, which had been constructed over the Kidron Valley. He retraced his steps along the same path he had used in riding the donkey in the triumphal entry a few days before. The Mount of Olives was beautiful and peaceful in the moonlight. The silent men reached the deep shade of the gnarled, ancient olive trees and followed Jesus into a quiet garden. They had often been here below, on a terrace near the mountain's base. It was called Gethsemane for "Olive Vat."

Simon Zealot brought up the rear of the little procession. He gripped one of the kitchen knives with anticipation. Bartholomew carried the second knife.

Jesus waited until the eleven were ringed around him in the garden. He spoke briefly, "Pray that you will not fall into temptation."

He moved off alone toward a place he had often gone before. The disciples stayed where they were and watched Jesus walk about a stone's throw where he knelt to pray. His anguished words came faintly to the disciples.

"Father, if you will, take this cup of suffering from me." Jesus seemed to hesitate, struggling with deep internal thoughts, before adding with finality, "Not my will, however, but your will be done."

It grew late. The disciples became sleepy. They sought comfortable positions against tree trunks and rocks and began to doze off as Jesus' solitary prayer continued.

His brow was soaked in beads of perspiration. As he prayed more and more earnestly, darker spots appeared like blood and mixed with the perspiration. The more intense Jesus' agony of prayer, the darker the bloody sweat became.

The disciples were asleep when faintly, from a distance, a woman shrieked. A babble of men's voices reacted to the woman's cry.

Across the valley, her words shrilled clearly. "Stop! Stop, murderer! Stop him!"

A man called, "You! Stop where you are! Stop, I say!"

Another male voice yelled, "I know that man! That's Barabbas!"

The woman screamed again. The babble of voices was momentarily lost in the determined running of nailed Roman sandal-boots.

The voices and the sounds died away, but none of the disciples had heard them. Jesus approached the group and looked down on them with stern disapproval.

"Why are you sleeping?"

The men stirred guiltily.

"Get up," Jesus commanded, "and pray that you will not fall into temptation."

Before they could rise, however, a body of the Temple police, scribes and priests rounded a corner of the garden. They moved with determination by the light of the torches held high. The disciples leaped to their feet, ready to flee, but the intruders silently blocked all escape. The lights reflected off sticks, staves, and a few naked swords.

Jesus stepped forward. Judas Iscariot's weasel eyes reflected a torch held by a Temple guard. The Judean seemed to recoil from Jesus, but Caiaphas and Annas were too close behind Judas for him to back up.

Judas stretched out his arms to embrace Jesus, who asked softly, "Judas, is it with a kiss that you betray the Son of Man?"

Judas recoiled, then crumpled to the ground, sobbing fitfully.

Bartholomew had tried to hide his knife behind his back. Simon Peter leaped forward, snatched the blade from loosened fingers, and swung the knife as a sword. It slashed down toward the head of a servant, standing next to the high priest. The servant ducked, his left ear was struck. Blood gushed in the torchlight.

Jesus cried, "Enough of this!"

He touched the servant's ear. The wound was instantly healed.

Those standing next to the man stirred uneasily. But Jesus' voice demanded the attention of everyone present. He spoke to Annas.

"Did you have to come with swords and clubs, as though I were an outlaw? I was with you in the Temple every day, and you did not try to arrest me!"

His voice changed. Resignedly, he said, "But this is your hour to act, when the power of darkness rules."

The high priest motioned for the Temple guards to seize Jesus. They grabbed him violently. He made no resistance. They began shouting and dragging Jesus roughly from the garden, ignoring the disciples. They found themselves suddenly free. They turned and fled into the night.

CHAPTER TWENTY-ONE

THE TORCHLIGHT procession crossed the Kidron Valley from the Mount of Olives, passed north of the Temple area, turned southward past the Antonia Fortress at the northwest corner, and moved down along the Temple's west wall by the Tyropean Valley. Lights passed the Hasmonean Palace just west of the Temple's royal portico area, and curled past the west of the upper city. The Temple guards in their light-gray uniforms conducted Jesus southwest between the lower city with the hippodrome and theater to the high priest's palaces. This was near the southwest corner of the Jerusalem's first wall.

Peter, watching the procession from a distance, saw the torchlights vanish into the courtyard of the high priest's home in the upper city. After a while, Peter entered the gate and joined some guards and women servants seated around a fire in the middle of the courtyard's earthen floor.

Peter glanced nervously around, watching the second-floor balcony, where a light burned inside a window. Jesus was probably being questioned there at night, in violation of all Sanhedrin rules.

Peter was conscious of a servant girl bending over him. He turned his bearded face up to her. She scrutinized him carefully and then turned to the noisy guards sitting around the fire.

"This man was with Jesus!"

Peter leaped up and backed away. "Woman, I don't even know him!"

The Temple guards and servants eyed Peter doubtfully. But none of the disciples had been taken prisoners with Jesus. The Captain of the Temple guard shrugged.

Inside the house, Jesus sat on the floor, bound with ropes. A dirty cloth had been roughly tied over his eyes. Four drunken Temple guards were poking at Jesus with clubs and the blunt end of their spears. As each blow landed, the guards laughed.

One guard smashed his club into Jesus' chest and demanded with wine-slurred voice, "Who hit you? Guess!"

Jesus said nothing.

A second guard cried, "Prophesy! Which one of us will strike you next?"

A scribe appeared with parchment and stylus. "Stop this! Bring him before the Council!"

The guards removed Jesus' blindfold and dragged

him into an adjoining room. Annas, Caiaphas, elders, and a captain of the Temple guard glared at him.

Annas, titular head of the religious hierarchy, stroked his gray beard.

"Tell us: are you the Messiah?"

Jesus looked at the old man. "If I tell you, you will not believe me, and if I ask you a question, you will not answer. But from now on, the Son of Man will be seated at the right hand of Almighty God."

Caiaphas demanded softly, "Are you, then, the Son of God?"

Jesus replied, "You say that I am."

The Council members were barely able to suppress their fury. A scribe from the sidelines exclaimed, "We ourselves have heard what he said!"

Caiaphas announced triumphantly, "We don't need any more witnesses!" The high priests' eyes gleamed with satisfaction. The first goal had been accomplished illegally. The next step would be harder.

In the courtyard below, Peter had resumed his seat among the servants and guards at the fire. Peter was afraid. He sat with head down, his eyes darting about. He saw that it was beginning to be light over the courtyard wall.

A man in the simple clothes of the people of the land peered at Peter through the smoke and said, "You are one of them, too!"

Peter denied it emphatically. "Man, I am not!"

The high priest's first-floor door swung open. All eyes turned to the sight of Jesus being led into the courtyard by the guards and Council members. They proceeded across the courtyard toward the outer gate.

At the fire, Peter felt someone grab his shoulder. The fisherman turned to see a male servant point. "There isn't any doubt that this man was with Jesus, because he also is a Galilean!"

Peter cried, "Man, I don't know what you are talking about!"

Before Peter's sentence was finished, a rooster crowed to welcome the dawn.

Jesus turned and looked at Peter.

He remembered Jesus' prediction, "Before the rooster crows tonight, you will say three times that you do not know me."

The fisherman leaped up, ran blindly across the courtyard away from Jesus. Peter shoved his way through the gate and out into the dawn, weeping bitterly.

It was not yet sunup when Jesus had been marched northeast again, along the west side of the Temple and around the north wall to the courtyard of Antonia Fortress.

Roman soldiers in golden helmets with the long ear protectors guarded the entrance. Only the chief priests, elders, and scribes were allowed to enter with Jesus. The Temple guards waited outside.

The legionnaires stood with their curved shields to their left, their long spears held in their right hands. Half-a-dozen cavalrymen with bright-red cloaks sat facing the second story of Pontius Pilate's official residence.

The governor appeared on the balcony. His puffy

face and paunch were in sharp contrast to his immaculate white toga. It was richly trimmed in royal purple. He hadn't been shaved yet this morning, and he was in a bad mood for having been awakened so early.

He approached the waist-high balcony railing marked with a crimson ruglike covering. He glowered down on the Jewish intruders. He raised fat hands, with a huge green stone on the left little finger. He wore a larger seal ring on his right forefinger.

The governor's baleful eyes settled on Jesus, whose face was beginning to show the effects of the physical abuse he'd taken.

"Tell me," Pilate said in an annoyed tone, "what has he done to command such urgency?"

Annas, the wily old priest who had served under Herod the king, had planned well. The Jewish Sanhedrin, the Council of seventy elders of which the high priest was the head, had no authority under the Romans to execute a man. The Council could condemn and find a man worthy of death, but it required the governor's sanction to execute capital punishment. The Romans had no interest in Jewish religious matters, so the official charge against Jesus would have to be a Roman offense, like sedition, to get an execution order.

Annas began, "We caught this man misleading our people."

Caiaphas added, "He was telling them not to pay taxes to the Emperor, and claiming that he himself is the Messiah; a king."

Pilate's sleepiness vanished. "A king?" The governor's eyes hardened, as they swept from the high priests to focus on Jesus. "Are you the king of the Jews?"

Jesus replied evenly, "So you say."

This answer infuriated the mob. They began calling out a chorus of accusations.

Pilate held up his pudgy hands for silence. He didn't want another riot. There had been earlier incidents, which had threatened his position with the emperor. Pilate recalled how he had brought the Roman soldiers' standards into the city. The Jews had protested the presence of these emblems with the Roman eagle, a symbol of idolatry. Pilate had been forced to remove the standards. Another time, he had been forced to back down when the Jews objected to his using certain Temple funds for an aqueduct to bring water to the capital city. One more complaint to the emperor, and Pilate could be banished.

When the crowd had settled down, and before Pilate could speak, Annas called up, "Sentence him, Pilate!"

Instantly, the crowd burst into angry support. "He's guilty! What will you proscribe?"

Again, the governor's fat hands came up to his flaccid face. He wasn't going to have a riot on his hands; neither was he going to allow himself to be used by the Jews over some point in their strange religious beliefs.

"I find no reason to condemn this man."

The mob was outraged. They yelled and made violent gestures, so that Pilate looked apprehensively at the Jews. He looked for reassurance from the cordon of foot soldiers and their glistening spear points. These legionnaires were backed up with the armed cavalrymen. Their long, red capes flowed gracefully down from their broad shoulders and across their mounts' haunches. It was ceremonial in appearance, but the horsemen were all proven veterans of war.

Pilate raised his hands for silence. Again, before he could speak, Caiaphas called out:

"With his teaching he is starting a riot among the people all through Judea!"

An elder yelled, "He caused an uproar in the Temple market!"

Annas added, "He began in Galilee, and now has come here."

It was a mistake to mention the northern province. Pilate seized on the information at once. He curled his thick fingers across the top of the railing and leaned forward with a hopeful gleam in his eyes.

"Is this man a Galilean?"

Pilate started to wait for an answer, then thought better of it. He didn't want to lose his opportunity to squirm out of the tight spot into which the Jewish religious hierarchy was pushing him. Pilate plunged on with a loud, relieved voice.

"Galilee is Herod's jurisdiction, so let Herod deal with him! Herod's still in Jerusalem!"

Herod Antipas, tetrarch of Galilee, had once yielded to his wife's demands for the death of John the Baptist. Jesus had once called Herod Antipas "that fox." Herod had come down from the north to Jerusalem for the Passover.

Pilate and Antipas had quarreled over some issue in

the past. As strong men with great power, each had considered the other at fault. So their rift had continued.

Perhaps the governor saw a way to be reconciled to the tetrarch. Perhaps Pilate simply wanted to share the blame, or pass the responsibility of Jesus' trial to another ruler. The governor's face didn't show which motivation, or both, had prompted his decision. But, obviously relieved at the simple solution, Pilate signaled his troops. The foot soldiers surrounded the prisoner. The governor turned and waddled along the covered balcony to the comfort of his quarters. That had been an easy solution to a touchy problem.

In a storehouse outside the city, a shaft of sunlight slipped through the open doorway to barely illuminate the unwindowed interior. Peter lay prostrate over some grain bags and bundles of rags.

Through his anguished tears, he raised his voice in penitent prayer.

"Lord, we beseech Thee, do as Thou art, in accordance with the Greatness of Thy power! Thou didst forgive our fathers in the times when they rebelled against Thy word. Thou wast angry with them—angry enough to destroy them; yet, through Thy love for them, and for Thy Covenant's sake, Thou didst spare them."

Jesus was surrounded by a cadre of Roman guards in Herod's palace, west and slightly south of the Temple.

Herod had received the news of Jesus' coming with mixed feelings. For a long time, the tetrarch had been hearing about Jesus. Herod hoped to see some miracle performed. He was also slightly apprehensive, for he wasn't quite sure who Jesus really was.

Herod's voice could be heard, as he approached the room where Jesus was being held. "I had John's head cut off, but who is this man I hear these things about?"

Herod entered the room and stopped, regarding Jesus with mixed emotions. The tetrarch was wearing a long purple robe with rich silver trim. The battered, bleeding prisoner, with his slightly soiled, simple robe contrasted sharply with the appearance of the ruler from Galilee.

Aware his Herodian guards and Roman soldiers were watching him, Herod circled Jesus, checking him critically. The two highest-ranked Jews, Annas, and Caiaphas, with other priests, elders, and scribes watched hopefully, until Herod had completed his inspection of the prisoner and stood facing him.

Herod demanded haughtily, "Who is it that you say you are?"

Jesus looked directly at Herod but did not reply.

Herod tried again. "Who are those that you call your disciples?"

Jesus remained silent.

Herod's face began to flush slightly. "It is said you can perform signs. Do something for me!"

Jesus said nothing.

Herod began to show his irritation. A slight murmur from the spectators disclosed that they were also getting impatient.

A priest broke the tension. "My lord, he has been

corrupting all the people! He calls himself a king."

It wasn't true; Jesus had never made such a claim. But what did it matter? The challenge to Herod's vanity was meant to rankle. Years ago he had gone to Rome to seek the crown of his late father, Herod the king, who had willed the title to Antipas's older brother, Archelaus. Archelaus had finally been named ethnarch by the emperor, and Herod Antipas had ended up with the lesser title of tetrarch of Galilee. But Herod Antipas had never forgotten that he had aspired to be king, and he didn't take kindly to the thought of someone in a simple robe claiming to be a king.

"This man a king?" The tetrarch finished another critical examination of Jesus. Herod started to laugh. The others joined him. The laughter encouraged Herod. Impulsively, he removed his royal purple robe and draped it over Jesus' shoulders. Herod stepped back and laughed heartily at the mockery he had accomplished in that simple motion. He motioned to a guard.

The Herodian soldier in a blue tunic with white piping on the sleeves reversed his spear and plunged the blunt end into Jesus' chest.

The blow bent Jesus forward at the waist. Two Roman soldiers behind Jesus kept him from moving back.

The Herodian soldier, pleased with the results of his first blow, repeated the process. Another soldier joined in the beating.

Jesus suffered in silence. Caiaphas and Annas exchanged satisfied glances. The crowd yelled encouragement, as the beating continued.

Finally, Herod tired of the soldiers' blows. Herod held up a restraining hand. The soldiers stopped, eyes gleaming with the savagery released against their bleeding, bruised, and mute prisoner.

The tetrarch waved a dismissal to the assembly. As they turned to leave, a Herodian soldier reached forward to remove the royal robe from Jesus' shoulders, but Herod shook his head.

"Send him back to Pilate," the tetrarch ordered. "This is his province."

The Roman soldiers and the Herodian troops seized Jesus and started out of the room. The mob, now excited by the sight of blood and Jesus' ignominious treatment, were bright-eyed with anticipation.

Herod called after Annas and Caiaphas, "And thank Pilate for such droll diversion!"

Jesus was dragged through Jerusalem's narrow, twisting streets toward the Antonia Fortress. Jesus' face was bleeding freely. His nose was swelling from a blow. There was an ugly blue bruise below his right eye. A few splashes of fresh blood had splattered on the royal robe Herod had given him.

Crowds had gathered in curiosity and fear. The soldiers roughly shoved the spectators aside. Behind them, a few frightened disciples followed, as Jesus was hustled back to another ordeal with Pilate.

CHAPTER TWENTY-TWO

PILATE WAS obviously angry. He wasn't, he told himself again, going to be used by these Jews over some point in their religion. He stood again on the balcony and waved the shouting crowd to silence. The Roman governor looked from the battered form of Jesus to the richly attired Annas and his son-in-law.

Pilate knew very well that the Jewish authorities had handed Jesus over to him because they were jealous. If Jesus were really the Jewish Messiah, he deserved to be arrested as a safeguard to the Roman authority which Pilate represented. But the governor hadn't seen anything seditious against the power he represented. Pilate goaded Caiaphas. "You brought this man to me and said that he was misleading the people. But I have not found him guilty of any of the crimes of which you accuse him."

The mob started to shout, but Pilate raised his voice and continued. "Nor did Herod find him guilty, for he sent him back to me. There is nothing this man has done to deserve death. So I will have him whipped and let him go."

Pilate folded his arms defiantly across his ample midsection. The crowd's outraged howl echoed around the courtyard.

Annas waited for the noise to subside, then he called up to the balcony. "You are obliged to release one man to us at this festival."

Pilate pursed his lips thoughtfully. The Jews and their Passover! Well, the custom of releasing one prisoner might work out well this time. There were several persons in custody, but the most logical prisoner to suggest was Barabbas. He was a robber and murderer. It would be a logical choice for the people to choose the inoffensive, bloody, and battered Jesus.

But Annas had thought carefully. As Pilate nodded in agreement, Annas moved to implement his plan. He called, "Away with Jesus, and release to us Barabbas!"

The crowd chimed in. "Barabbas! We want Barabbas!"

Pilate's pudgy hands came up in protest. This was starting to get out of hand. He called down to Annas and Caiaphas, "But what crime has he committed? I can't find that he has done anything to deserve death."

The crowd's derision started to swell upward from the courtyard, but Pilate yelled louder.

"I will have him whipped and set free!"

"No!" The crowd's roar hit Pilate with the force of an unexpected blow. He stepped back in surprise.

Caiaphas knew his timing. He cupped his old hands against his gray-bearded mouth and shouted, "Crucify him!"

The mob snatched up the word and began to chant. "Crucify! Crucify! Crucify him!"

The crowd was becoming unruly. They surged forward, ignoring the half-dozen red-caped cavalrymen and the cordon of armed foot legionnaires. They shifted uneasily but held their places.

Pilate shouted something but his voice was lost in the rising crescendo of mob anger. Jesus was momentarily ignored, as the mob's fury was turned venomously upon the Roman ruler. In another moment, the hostility would be unleashed against the soldiers. They'd retaliate. News of the resulting riot would surely reach Rome. This time, Caesar Tiberius might act against the governor who could not keep order in his province.

"Very well!" Pilate bowed his head and the crowd cheered at his submission. "In a moment, you shall have your crucifixion order."

The crowd swirled about impatiently, until Pilate returned to the balcony. He threw the rolled parchment down. A scribe seized it and handed it to Annas. He grabbed the document and held it high. The triumphant antagonists waved and yelled as a cadre of soldiers seized Jesus and hurried him roughly across the courtyard.

In the prison beneath the fortress a burly guard with

a ring of keys and accompanied by two Roman soldiers clomped noisily down the echoing, dreary corridor. They stopped before a cell door.

Barabbas, in rags, drew back against the moist, stone wall.

One of the soldiers snorted, as the guard opened the door. "The governor has released you according to the custom at the feast, Barabbas!"

Doubtfully, the ragged prisoner moved forward to the heavy iron gate. "Released *me*?"

The guard motioned with his thumb. "Out! And be thankful that it's Jesus of Nazareth they're going to crucify instead of you!"

The Passover crowd was thick in Jerusalem's narrow streets. The annual spring festival always brought countless thousands from everywhere. But the word that Jesus was to be crucified had raced through the city. People had left their homes or tents to flock together, wherever they might get a glimpse of this man about whom they'd heard so much.

Jesus was to die with two other condemned men. Each bloody man, suffering from the scourging, was forced to carry the *patibulum*, or shorter horizontal part of the cross through the city streets and outside the walls, where the posts which completed the cross awaited their victims.

This was a somber, silent crowd, totally unlike the religious hierarchy's coached cronies, who had badgered a Roman governor into submitting again to their massed wills. The crowd lining Jerusalem's street leading to the city's north gate was not entirely mute, in grief, however. Some always had to jeer the condemned.

A brutal-faced Roman centurion preceded the procession of condemned. A three-foot-long hardwood truncheon, covered with leather and weighted at the end, swept all spectators aside.

Behind him, four Roman soldiers in cardinal tunics used their curved shields to push the crowd back. The first condemned man was short-haired with a sparse dark beard. His neck was bent forward, so a heavy weathered crossbeam rested on his naked shoulders. Four ropes crossed his biceps and encircled the wooden beam. Two large iron circles dangled at the end of the beams.

Behind him, four more soldiers marched with spears at the ready. Jesus staggered along behind them, his bloody, sweaty face partially lost under his long, dark hair.

Behind Jesus, four more legionnaires kept the crowd back. The third condemned man brought up the rear. He had slightly longer hair than the first criminal. He was also fairly young and strong enough so that he did not stumble under his crossbeam.

But Jesus had been beaten, punched, slapped and then flayed with the dreaded Roman flagellum. This cruel whip had an eighteen-inch-long handle terminating in leather thongs. Imbedded in each thong were a number of sheep knucklebones or pieces of metal. Each time one of the dumbbell-shaped bones had bitten into his skin, the flesh had been more than ripped open; it had been mangled.

His own simple robe had been roughly pulled down across the horribly torn body, and, as the blood coagulated, the garment adhered to each spot. Every movement tore open the wounds with excruciating agony.

Jesus sagged to his knees under the weakness of suffering and weight of the crossbeam. Sympathetic women reached out to help, but menacing Roman spear points drove them back.

Soldiers roughly jerked Jesus to his feet. He staggered on amidst the jeers of the few and the sounds of loud wailing from lamenting women.

Jesus fell a second time landing on the side of his face. An old woman boldly leaned forward and tipped a water pitcher from her shoulder to his lips. He tried to smile, but his cracked, bruised lips wouldn't permit such a simple thing. A Roman jabbed menacingly at the old woman, but she ignored him and held the water pitcher to Jesus' lips, until he pulled back.

Again yanked to his feet, Jesus staggered on but fell almost immediately. Unable to break his fall with his hands, his face smashed into the rocky street. The nearest Roman drew his short sword and swung it hard in a flashing silver arc. The keen blade severed all four ropes holding Jesus' arms to the crossbeam. It rolled heavily down his back and stopped in the small of his back.

The centurion approached and glanced at Jesus'

battered body and his bleeding face. The centurion's plumed helmet glistened, as he turned to the crowd and singled out a tall, strong-looking man.

"You!" The centurion's heavy voice smashed aside the spectators in front of the man. "Step over here! What's your name?"

The bewildered man nervously brushed his young, luxurious beard. "Me? Simon, sir. Simon of Cyrene...."

"Pick it up, Cyrenian!"

The centurion's truncheon thumped heavily on the solid crossbeam. Two legionnaires handed their weapons and shields to their companions. The soldiers helped lift the crossbeam to Simon's shoulders. They lashed the beam onto his arms.

Jesus painfully raised himself to his knees. He looked around at the wailing women and forced his cracked lips to form words.

"Women of Jerusalem! Don't cry for me, but for yourselves and your children. For if such things as these are done when the wood is green, what will happen when it is dry?"

The women weren't quite sure what Jesus meant. They glanced uncertainly at each other, as the legionnaires prodded Jesus to his feet with spears and shoved him ahead of them.

Jesus went on, followed by Simon, bearing his crossbeam through the gate and along a dirt road outside the city.

The wailing women followed the sad procession to a place called in Latin *Calvarius*, or Calvary; the

Hebrews called the place "Golgotha." Both words meant "the skull."

The Jews never executed by crucifixion. Only the Romans used this form of capital punishment with a history that went back for centuries. The Persians, Phoenicians, and Carthaginians had used the method. The Romans executed so many people that holes were permanently dug into the ground outside Jerusalem. The upright beams had been laid flat beside the holes, in preparation for the next victims. Each post had a *sedicula*, a sort of ledge on which victims barely sat. The condemned men's crossbeams were lashed into place to form crosses.

Rough hands stripped the victims naked and tossed the three condemned men's clothes into separate piles near the crosses. Jesus, in the center, and the two criminals were forced onto their backs, on top of the crossbeams. Their arms were pulled out along each rough *patibulum*.

Experienced legionnaires reached into leather buckets and pulled out three six-inch-long spikes for each victim. The condemned men, facing up to a spring sky, had their hands seized and held palms up. They could hear the wailing women and the soldiers shouting.

A spike was placed against Jesus' right wrist in a manner proven effective over hundreds of years. Nailed palms would not support a man's weight. Jesus glimpsed the heavy iron hammer as it lifted and smashed down.

The nail shot through the small blood vessels and

tissue, finding the area where four tiny bones met. This space yielded to the plunging nail point. It went through, pushing the small bones aside, and entering the crossbeam. The sensitive nerves were torn as the spike ripped through the wrist.

The women turned away from the gruesome sight. The other wrist was quickly secured. The proficient soldiers, used to daily crucifixions, placed Jesus' right foot on top of the left. Again, the heavy metal flashed down. The single spike smashed through both feet and into the bottom of the post. It had taken only three blows of the great hammers.

Deftly, the Romans placed slipped ropes through the rusted iron rings at the end of Jesus' crossbeam. Other soldiers cursingly guided the base of the longer post into the hole. With a chorus of encouragement to each other, the soldiers pulled on the ropes. Jesus' cross rose ponderously into the air. The olive wood vertical post slid into the hole dug in the ground. Jesus' body sagged heavily against the wrist nails. His hips barely rested on the *sedicula*. The foot nail resisted the body weight.

Stones and pieces of wood were driven into the ground beside the post to keep it steady and upright. At a command, the ropes used to raise the cross released. They were quickly pulled through the iron rings. The loose rope ends fell to the rocky ground. A young soldier gathered the ropes into a coil.

The soldiers repeated the process with the two criminals. Then the Romans stepped back to examine their work.

Three crosses stood upright against the morning sky.

The three naked men sagged heavily by their arms. Screams of agony from the writhing men made women spectators turn away. The soldiers wanted a drink. It was easier to crucify a man, if the executions were numbed with wine. Sometimes it took a week to die. Mercifully, death sometimes came sooner. The wounds each man had received were not necessarily fatal, but the prolonged torture from every source made a crucifixion victim long for the release of death.

The pain of mangled flesh from the scourging and the pain of the nails were only part of the torture. The *sedicula* was designed to allow a man just enough resting on the tip of his hips to extend his agony. Thirst was a vital reality. So were the insects attracted by the bloody wounds and the victims' inability to resist their attacks. Exposure to the sun and other elements, the terrible inability to move except in a very restricted way because of the rigid position, and the jeering, taunting words of spectators added to the torture and humiliation.

Death came by exposure and pain. But the approach of death was usually so slow that even the rabbis were uncertain when a crucified man was legally dead. A legal ruling was finally determined: the crucified man was dead when vultures began feeding on his vital organs.

That was what awaited Jesus and the two men hanging between earth and sky on either side of him. The two criminals writhed in excruciating agony, screamed at the top of their voices, or moaned with the deep, terrible pain, which was just beginning.

Nearby, among the large mass of people fanned out across the flat area at the base of the slope, the keening women covered their faces with their shawls and sobbed loudly.

But there were other spectators who regarded the three crosses—and especially the one in the center—with grim satisfaction.

CHAPTER TWENTY-THREE

THE ROMAN SOLDIERS had become fairly hardened to seeing men die by crucifixion, but it was best to be kept busy, while waiting for their victims to die.

The centurion turned away from the crosses and held up Jesus' robe. It was a simple garment, woven without a seam, but devoid of ornamentation. The centurion tossed the robe toward the soldiers. The youngest caught it and clutched it to himself, but the others demanded an opportunity to have it. The young soldier shrugged, threw the garment on the rocky ground, and produced some dice.

"This is no ordinary mystic's robe," he announced. "This belongs to the King of the Jews himself. High number wins it. Agreed?"

Another soldier cried, "It's a fine royal robe. I'm going to win it for myself."

The soldiers fell eagerly to their knees and began

throwing the dice onto the robe. Annas stood thoughtfully looking up at the center cross. Then he appraised the mixed crowd of mourners and jeering men and said softly to his son-in-law, "He saved others. Let him save himself—*if* he is the Messiah whom God has chosen."

A spectator, torn between his desire to believe and the fact that Jesus was nailed to the cross, yelled in a broken, trembling voice through cupped hands, "Save yourself—if you are the King of the Jews!"

Jesus raised his head with great difficulty and turned his face to the sky.

"Forgive them, Father! They don't know what they are doing."

With the embarrassment which comes in the face of death and not knowing what else to do, some spectators laughed. They hooted and jeered, pointing up at the center cross in derision.

But some of the spectators were silent in their grief. Even the women had stopped sobbing so loudly, as they watched in muted grief at the tragedy being unfolded in front of their eyes.

The crucifixion squad turned to their wine, as three more Roman soldiers marched up the slope from Jerusalem. One carried a large jar of vinegar for the condemned men. The second legionnaire gripped a rough piece of wood on which something had been hastily written in Greek, Latin, and Hebrew.

The new soldiers mocked Jesus, as they picked up the ladder and placed it against the center cross. One climbed up to Jesus' left with a nail hammer and the sign. The soldier nailed the sign above Jesus' head.

Pilate had sent up the sign with Jesus' crime rudely scrawled on it.

The spectators plainly saw the wording: THIS IS THE KING OF THE JEWS.

One of the other newly arrived soldiers soaked a sponge in the cheap wine, put it on the end of a stick and thrust it up to Jesus' mouth. Crucifixion caused great thirst. Jesus tasted the wine but wouldn't drink. He closed his mouth tightly and turned his face away. The liquid ran down his beard and mixed with the intensely heavy perspiration on his chest.

The soldier who'd nailed the sign over Jesus' head surveyed his handiwork with satisfaction. He started backing down the ladder, nodding mockingly to Jesus and saying, "Majesty!"

The other soldiers jeered, holding up their own wine. The centurion thumped his heavy truncheon thoughtfully into his open left palm and looked carefully at Jesus' bloody, sweat-drenched face.

The short-haired younger crucifixion victim on Jesus' left spoke with great difficulty and bitterness. "Aren't you the Messiah? Save yourself and us!"

The other criminal turned to look at the speaker.

"Don't you fear God?" he demanded of his companion. "You received the same sentence he did. Ours, however, is only right because we are getting what we deserve for what we did, but he has done no wrong." The penitent man turned his eyes to Jesus, "Remember me, Jesus, when you come as King!"

Jesus said softly, "I promise you that today you will be in Paradise with me."

Suddenly, all the spectators glanced apprehensively at the sky. It was the Passover season, which meant a full moon, so there could be no eclipse. But the sky was starting to get dark. Yet, it was noon on a day that had been entirely clear, there were no clouds in the sky.

In the Antonia Fortress, Joseph of Arimathea blinked in surprise at the mysteriously darkening sky. The Roman soldiers kept their military stance with shields and spears, but their eyes were also on the sky.

Pilate walked briskly into the courtyard and faced Joseph. "What is it?" the governor demanded.

"My lord, I have prepared a grotto for the teacher, Jesus. By your leave, I will consign his body to the tomb."

Pilate pursed his puffy lips. Sometimes he could command a price for allowing a crucified man's body to be ransomed for burial. But Pilate had enough of the whole business for one day.

He shrugged, nodded affirmatively, and walked away, saying, "I'll send out the order."

Joseph of Arimathea was still standing where Pilate had left him, when suddenly the sun was totally obscured. The darkness fell like a great blanket.

Pilate stopped abruptly and glanced apprehensively upward. The soldiers shifted their weapons uneasily and cut their eyes to look beyond their helmets at the rapidly darkening sky.

The shadow's lip swept across the city's wall, raced across the Temple courtyard and touched the great double doors of the sanctuary.

Inside, the great blue veil, which separated the holy

place from the Holy of Holies, suddenly ripped in half and sagged to the sides.

The shadow sped on, silently engulfing the rest of the Temple grounds, then slid rapidly across the city wall and arrived at the crucifixion site.

Jesus raised his head and cried out with surprising power, "Father! into your hands place my spirit!"

Jesus' head fell forward. His body sagged lifelessly against the three nails.

The centurion at the foot of the center cross looked at the still figure, removed his plumed helmet in an instinctive gesture, and whispered:

"Glory be to God! Certainly he was a good man!"

The darkened sky drove the jeering and mourning people alike into a somber silence. With one accord, all stared at the threatening darkness of noon. Fearfully, some began hurrying toward their homes. But Joanna, Mary Magdalene, and Susanna, with some of the apostles stood, mutely back from the cross, watching in baffled grief and awe as the darkness seemed to thicken over the whole area.

For three hours, the intense, unexplained darkness continued.

The three women, with some of their companions who had accompanied Jesus from Galilee, were still there when the sky slowly returned to normal three hours later. The same women kept their vigil, until a normal sundown approached. Then they stirred, for the Sabbath was approaching.

The Roman soldiers moved methodically to the criminal on Jesus' right.

There was a thud of a heavy hammer and the scream of the anguished man, as his legs were broken. His entire weight was thrown onto his nailed wrists. He could no longer use his legs for support. His biceps and shoulders alone were to carry his weight.

The soldier hefted his mallet and came to Jesus. It was surprising to see that he was already dead. The soldier moved to the third man and methodically broke his legs.

A spear was jabbed upward into Jesus' chest to make sure he was dead.

Joseph of Arimathea passed the waiting women and approached the centurion.

"I have permission from the governor...."

The soldier glanced briefly at the scroll which the merchant handed him. He nodded. "Take him," he said. He motioned for legionnaires to lower Jesus' body.

Nearby in a new garden tomb, Joseph's servant unrolled a long length of fine new linen. When Jesus' body was brought to the grotto, Joseph of Arimathea took over. He tenderly wrapped the corpse and stepped back. He nodded to his servant, who bent at Jesus' head and helped Joseph carry the body into the tomb, which had been recently cut out of the limestone rock.

It was a large family sepulchre, with a few rough steps leading down into a larger room. Niches along both sides and at the far end provided shelves with low ceilings. Jesus' corpse was gently laid at the far end on a rock shelf. Joseph of Arimathea stepped back to take one last look. Satisfied, he bent to the earthen floor and picked up a handful of dirt. Gently but deliberately, he sprinkled it lightly and symbolically on his own head in a mark of grief.

As he passed tearfully out the entrance, four husky soldiers joined the servant in rolling the great stone over the tomb's entrance. Like a monstrous millstone on end, the stone crunched ponderously in the groove cut for it.

Joseph stood watching through eyes flooded with tears of grief, until the stone thudded solidly into place. The tomb was closed.

A woman's voice behind Joseph of Arimathea said softly, "Forgive us...."

He turned to see Mary Magdalene, Joanna, and Susanna. Their own tear-streaked faces testified to their deep grief.

Mary explained brokenly, "We came to see where you laid our Lord. When the Sabbath is over, we will return with the spices."

Joseph nodded. "I understand. But come; we must hurry, for the sun is almost down."

They walked heavily away from the garden tomb, just as the sound of the *shofar* signaled the Sabbath.

Darkness quickly settled over the tomb where Jesus of Nazareth, aged about thirty-three, was crucified, dead and buried. The hopes of many people lay entombed with him.

CHAPTER TWENTY-FOUR

SOME THIRTY-SIX hours later, just before dawn after the Sabbath, the women returned to the tomb. Mary Magdalene, Joanna, Susanna and Mary, the mother of James made their way along the stony path. The women carried small jars of prepared spices, boxes or flasks of ointments, and rolled strips of white linen.

They rounded a rock face close to the tomb and stopped in astonishment. The great stone had been rolled aside. Exchanging bewildered glances, the women cautiously approached. Mary Magdalene bent and peered nervously inside.

In the light from the open tomb, she could see that Jesus' body was not there. "They've taken him away!" She exclaimed.

The other women pushed their way carefully to where they could see down into the tomb at the far end.

The burial cloth was faintly visible on the rock ledge.

It retained the shape of the corpse, but sagged with obvious emptiness.

Susanna started down the stairs for a closer look at the shroud.

Mary Magdalene reached out to stop Joanna, but a sudden brilliant flash of intense white light filled the grotto. The women drew back in fear as two shining figures stood between them and the back wall where the corpse had lain.

The women were terrified. They instantly prostrated themselves before the incandescence of the two men.

The women heard one ask with gentle reproof, "Why are you looking among the dead for one who is alive?"

The women stole furtive glances up at the speaker. He continued, "He is not here; he has been raised."

The women didn't know what to say, but they cautiously raised their heads toward the men. The second one spoke.

"Remember what he said to you while he was in Galilee: 'The Son of Man must be handed over to sinful men, be crucified, and three days later rise to life.'"

These words were too much for the three women. They dropped their spices and scrambled out of the grotto, clutching each other in fear and hope and surprise. They hurried back down the path.

They burst into the storehouse, where Peter had fled to weep after he had denied knowing Jesus. The eleven apostles, minus Judas Iscariot, had come here to sit in sackcloth and grieve. The disciples looked up in startled concern at the women.

Joanna was breathless but managed to exclaim, "Listen! We were at the Lord's tomb when two men—angels—appeared before us."

The disciples showed skepticism, as Joanna continued to blurt out her report. "They were shining like the sun, and said to us, 'Why do you look for the living among the dead?'"

The disciples exchanged sad glances. It was obvious they didn't believe Joanna.

Mary Magdalene seized Peter's tunic sleeve with great conviction. "It's true! The stone was rolled away, so we entered and—and the body of our Lord—was gone!"

The men shook their heads in disbelief. The women chorused, "It's true! Believe us! He has risen, just as he said!"

Peter and John exchanged looks. They examined the face of the three earnest, radiantly happy women. Impulsively, Peter leaped up and headed for the door.

John raced after him, passed the bigger man in a few strides, and sped on through the morning toward the tomb.

But inside the storehouse, the other nine disciples sadly shook their heads and refused to believe the women.

That afternoon, Cleopas and another disciple were walking along a rocky road toward Emmaus, a village about seven miles from Jerusalem. A donkey and cart passed them going toward Jerusalem. A tent was pitched alongside the road and pretty yellow flowers bloomed beside the road. But the two travelers didn't notice.

Their eyes were swollen and red from weeping. Their steps were slow and weary with grief. They hardly noticed a man with his face hidden inside his cowl who fell into step beside them.

The newcomer asked, "What are you talking about to each other as you walk along?"

Cleopas brushed a weary hand across his eyes. "Are you the only visitor to Jerusalem who doesn't know the things that have been happening there these last few days?"

"What things?"

The two men looked at each other in surprise.

Cleopas replied to the stranger's question. "The things that happened to Jesus of Nazareth."

The other disciple explained, "This man was a prophet and was considered by God and by all the people to be powerful in everything he said and did."

The stranger listened to the disciples' sad recitation of the events which had led to Jesus' death and the women's report of the empty tomb.

Cleopas concluded, "Some of our group went to the tomb and found it exactly as the women had said, but they did not see him."

The stranger exclaimed, "How foolish you are, how slow you are to believe everything the prophets said! Was it not necessary for the Messiah to suffer these things and then to enter his glory?"

The stranger began to explain the Scriptures so clearly that the two disciples understood what was written about the Messiah, from the books of Moses through the writing of all the prophets.

The stranger was still talking when the three men came to an intersection near the village. The newcomer raised his hand in farewell. He started to walk straight ahead, as the disciples turned to the right. Then Cleopas hurried after him and brought him back. The three walked on toward Emmaus.

That night, in a village house, the stranger reclined alone at a low table. The two disciples entered the room with wine and cups, bread and meat. Cleopas poured the wine, while the other disciple set the food on the table. Then the men also reclined.

Their companion picked up the bread, broke it in two and said, "Blessed art Thou, O Lord our God, King of the Universe, Who bringeth forth bread from the earth."

The realization that this companion was Jesus hit both disciples at once. Cleopas prostrated himself in fear, but the other leaped up and backed away in terror, his hands covering his eyes.

When the disciples had the courage to look again, Jesus was gone. The wine and broken bread were still on the table.

Cleopas was still trembling. "Wasn't it like a fire burning in us when he talked to us on the road and explained the Scriptures to us?"

At the Jerusalem storehouse the next night, ten disciples, the women and about a dozen others were gathered for dinner. They were finishing a meal of fish, bread, fruit, and honeycomb, when James rushed in, trailed by Cleopas and the other disciple of the Emmaus Road experience.

James cried in great excitement. "The Lord is risen indeed! He has appeared to Simon!"

Cleopas exclaimed, "We didn't recognize him . . . not on the road. . . ."

The other Emmaus Road disciple broke in, "But when he broke the bread, *then* we knew!"

Susanna frowned. "At Emmaus? How strange that Jesus should go there."

Cleopas ventured a guess. "Perhaps there is no place he would not go."

The people were so intent on the report that no one noticed an addition to their company. James, son of Zebedee, suddenly glanced up and let out an exclamation. The others turned silently to see what had grasped his attention.

Jesus had suddenly and mysteriously appeared in the back of the room. He spoke softly.

"Shalom. Peace be with you."

The little company was terrified. They shrank back as though they were seeing a ghost.

Jesus smiled at them and extended his hands. "Why are you alarmed? Why are these doubts coming up in your minds?"

When no one moved, Jesus moved forward and extended his hands.

"Look at my hands and my feet, and see that it is I, myself. Feel me, and you will know, for a ghost doesn't have flesh and bones, as you see I have."

Bartholomew found enough courage to cautiously extend his right hand and gingerly touch Jesus. But the others were still drawn back in fear and wonder. Expressions of confusion and joy chased each other across their faces until Jesus spoke again.

"Do you have anything here to eat?"

Susanna broke out of her trance. She moved to the rounded oven in the back corner of the room and returned with some broiled fish. Jesus took it, gave thanks, and began to eat.

Everyone stared at Jesus in confusion. Even Bartholomew seemed unsure, staring wordlessly at his own hands, which had touched Jesus. Bartholomew had seen Jesus' wounds, which were still visible but totally healed.

Jesus put down his piece of fish and spoke again.

"These are the very things I told you about while I was with you: everything written about me in the Law of Moses, the writings of the prophets, and the Psalms had to come true."

Jesus paused, looking around the room with great patience at the disciples and women, who did not fully grasp what had happened, and what Jesus was saying. He continued:

"This is what is written: 'the Messiah must suffer and must rise from death three days later, and in his name the message about repentance and the forgiveness of sins must be preached to all nations, beginning in Jerusalem."

The next day, Jesus led the little band from Jerusalem

to Bethany, a couple miles outside the capital. They walked behind him through a windy field. There he stopped, gathered the men and women about him, and looked lovingly at each of them before speaking.

Jesus' time was short. He had taught them for three years before his crucifixion. In his post-resurrection state he had explained the Scriptures so the disciples now understood about the Resurrection. He had given them His commands, and what they must do until he came again. They were to be his witnesses in all the world. But they would need more than their own strength to do what seemed an impossible task. Jesus spoke quietly, "And I myself will send upon you what my Father has promised."

Jesus paused, looking from one to another with searching eyes to make sure each understood what he was doing. The risen Christ was entrusting these few with reaching generations yet unborn, plus uncounted millions of people down through the centuries. He knew they could not do it alone.

"But you must wait in the city until the power from above comes down on you," he cautioned.

Jesus held out his arms. The little band of faithful men and women gathered tightly about him.

A heavy wind whipped the area. The disciples struggled to keep their eyes upon Jesus, as he raised his arms over them in benediction.

"The Lord bless you and keep you. . . ."

The disciples and women collectively let out a little gasp of surprise, as Jesus slowly began ascending vertically from their midst.

As Jesus rose higher into the air, the people sank reverentially to their knees, their heads uplifted, eyes following his ascent, higher and higher.

Jesus became a tiny dot in the sky and then vanished into a cloud. The little band of faithful followers were still staring toward heaven when two men in white suddenly stood beside them.

The women and the disciples blinked in surprise. The two men in white spoke as one, their words so close together they were not echoes, but one voice with double emphasis.

"Galileans, why are you standing there looking up at the sky? This Jesus, who was taken from you into heaven, will come back in the same way that you saw him go to heaven."

The apostles understood. Jesus was coming again! In the meantime, they had a divine commission. They must return to Jerusalem, wait for the power of the Holy Spirit, and then go out into the whole world and tell people about Jesus who was dead, buried, and risen again, so that all who believe in him may also have everlasting life.

All that was nearly two thousand years ago. The disciples have long gone to be with Jesus. But they have passed the Great Commission down through the generations—to this very hour—to us.

We, too, have a divine commission. It's time we were up and doing. For this same Jesus is coming again. And it may be soon.

Epilogue

Then he opened their minds to understand the Scriptures, and said to them, "This is what is written: the Messiah must suffer and must rise from death three days later, and in his name the message about repentance and the forgiveness of sins must be preached to all nations, beginning in Jerusalem. You are witnesses of these things. And I myself will send upon you what my Father has promised. But you must wait in the city until the power from above comes down upon you."

Then he led them out of the city as far as Bethany, where he raised his hands and blessed them. As he was blessing them, he departed from them and was taken up into heaven. They worshiped him and went back into Jerusalem, filled with great joy.

Luke 24:45–52

SOME FACTS ABOUT THE FILM

I   *The Script*

The script for the film was taken almost entirely from the Gospel of Saint Luke. It is presented without editorial comment.

Jesus speaks no words other than those found in the New Testament.

The text is taken largely from the *Good News Bible (TEV)*, formerly known as *Good News for Modern Man*, translation. This contemporary translation lends itself most readily to the spoken word. Some of the more familiar parts of Saint Luke, however, such as The Lord's Prayer and The Beatitudes, are taken from the King James translation in the film.

More than two hundred scholars checked the

script to ensure its historical and biblical accuracy.

The script has been endorsed by several hundred key leaders, representing every major denomination and parachurch organization.

II. *The Producer*

The producer is the Genesis Project, a New York-based company. President John Heyman has produced more than thirty major motion pictures and has been involved in the financing of an additional fifty films.

He read law at Oxford University and then entered the film industry.

He won the Cannes Film Festival with *The Hireling* and *The Go-Between*.

He became one of Britain's top film agents. His clients included Elizabeth Taylor, Richard Burton, Richard Harris, Trevor Howard, Shirley Bassey, Andre Previn, and Burt Bacharach.

He began working in 1969 on the concept of translating the Bible onto film. In 1974, he organized the Genesis Project to realize that desire. The result: *The New Media Bible*, a 20-year $200-million-dollar project.

III. *The Cast and Crew*

The directors are:

John Krish. Krish is one of the most acclaimed international prize-winning directors. His productions include: *Let My People Go, I Think They Call Him John,* and *The First Line.* He was the original director of the television series "The Avengers." He is resident scholar on filmmaking for British Broadcasting Company films. These films include *Unearthly Stranger, Decline and Fall,* and *Man Who Had Power Over Woman.*

Peter Sykes. Sykes is Peter Brooks's assistant at the Royal Shakespearian Company. He directed sixteen documentaries on the World's Fair, "Expo '67," in Montreal. His films include five of the Orson Welles Great Mystery Series. Other features include: *The Quester, Wipeout, Walkabout, Die Laughing, The House in Nightmare Park,* and *Steptoe Rides Again* (on which was based the television series, "Sanford and Son").

The cast is primarily composed of Israelis and Arabs. An attempt was made to be as authentic as possible in the selection of the cast and extras. "To find 5000 people with 2000-year-old faces," the casting director turned to the Jews from the Middle East. Their features appear to be unchanged from their ancestors of the first century.

Jesus is played by English Shakespearian actor
Brian Deacon. Deacon has worked relentlessly on
the difficult task of portraying Jesus. Deacon said,
"Every day, when I go to the set to portray Jesus, I
realize how mortal I am." He has done a superb
job of depicting a manly, virile, compassionate
Christ. During the filming, the extras would
sometimes break into spontaneous applause
following one of the sermons of Deacon's Jesus.
Deacon memorized whole chapters of Saint
Luke's Gospel, reading the book through twenty-
two times in the two weeks before shooting
began.

Herodias is played by Deacon's wife, Countess
Rula Lenska.

IV. *The Scenes and Sets*

Research on the dress, customs, and food of the
time of Christ has been underway for over five
years. What researchers discovered greatly
affected filming. For example, the filmmakers
had to be careful not to film any eucalyptus
trees, since they did not exist in Israel until 1934.

Locations were chosen as close as possible to the
original sites, where the action was believed to
have taken place. In some places, television
antennas and telephone poles had to be temporar-
ily removed, so they would not appear in the
background.

Many of the scenes were shot in Arab villages on the West Bank of the Jordan River, through the courteous cooperation of both the Palestinians who live there, and the Israeli government.

The sets cost over $1 million. The set designers rebuilt the Temple, as well as three synagogues and a fleet of fishing boats. The fish used in the scene of the miraculous draft of the fish in Peter's boat were actually caught by local fishermen in the Sea of Galilee.

V.   *Luke, the Gospel Writer*

What do we know of this man personally?

We get few clues from his writings. He said very little about himself, in order to glorify God through Jesus Christ. Luke's deeply moving writing technique is unique in the Scriptures, yet this is only a bonus—an extension of the man's own personality.

From the letters of Paul the Apostle, we know that Luke was "our dear doctor." In the final days of Paul's life, shortly before he was martyred in Rome about A.D. 64, the prisoner Paul wrote the stirring testimony to Luke's faithfulness: "Only Luke is with me."

Luke accompanied Paul on some of his missionary trips to the Gentiles. Therefore, Luke knew firsthand about many of the later events. He wrote about these in the Book of Acts. Yet Luke had not personally known what had happened in the very beginning of Jesus' story, starting with the angel's visit to Zechariah the priest. Zechariah was to become the father of John the Baptist. Luke had no firsthand information about the annunciation to Mary; of the birth of the Christ Child in the cave-stable at Bethlehem. Luke had not been present when the angels announced to the shepherds that a Savior had been born; nor was Luke present when John began baptizing, and Jesus presented himself as a candidate for baptism.

Luke had to depend on research for those events, plus all those others which happened before he came into the picture. After many interviews with eyewitnesses and careful research, he began writing a letter—the only medium available to him at that time. He used what God had provided as a communications tool to report about the events which had shaken the world and would continue to shake it for centuries to come. As the only non-Jewish New Testament writer—and as an educated Greek with an outsider's perspective—Luke could be both reporter and feature writer about the most important events ever recorded in this history of the world.

Luke put his reputation on the line for thousands of years by writing accurately—and vividly—of historical personages and events, which could be verified or challenged by later scholars. Luke wrote chronologically in the methodical, studied practice of the skilled scientist of his time. This physician-writer has left us a wonderful heritage: the story of the greatest Man who ever lived.

TELL US WHAT FILMS YOU WOULD LIKE TO SEE!

FILM VIEWERS SURVEY

You can help us decide which worthwhile and responsible films we produce in the future. Please check which films you would most like to see. We'll give your response our most serious consideration.

	1st Choice	2nd Choice	3rd Choice	Not Interested
Acts of the Apostles				
Paul the Apostle				
Revelation				
A Severe Mercy				
The Burning Book (Tyndale)				
The Persecutor				
Christy				
Other				

Topics or ideas _____

Please complete and mail to:

> J. D. Kenneth Bliss
> Inspirational Film Distributors, Inc.
> 1911 S. Commercenter East, Suite 111
> San Bernardino, CA 92408

☐ Please let me know when future films will be
   shown in my community
☐ Please keep me informed of your progress in
   translating and distributing *Jesus* overseas.

NAME _____

ADDRESS _____

CITY _____ STATE _____ ZIP ____

INCREASE YOUR UNDERSTANDING OF SCRIPTURE

What Gutenberg did in the fifteenth century the Genesis Project aims to do today—use the most up-to-date technology to bring the Bible to more people. This nondenominational organization has put the Bible on film—the vital medium of the twentieth century—and produced The New Media Bible.

The New Media Bible is a series of rich and dramatic color films shot entirely on location in Israel. Authentic costumes, sets, and artifacts bring Scripture to life for Bible study groups everywhere—in churches, schools, hospitals, and even prisons.

The films are accompanied by magazines, filmstrips, teacher's guides, projectionist's scripts, and cassettes. All the components are designed to make The New Media Bible a comprehensive Bible education program.

USE THE NEW MEDIA BIBLE.

CLIP THE COUPON BELOW FOR FURTHER INFORMATION ON HOW YOUR CHURCH CAN OWN ONE.